SIDE by SIDE

Extra

Book & eText **1**

Expanded Grammar

Self-Tests & Skill Checks

Digital FunZone & Audio

Steven J. Molinsky • Bill Bliss

Illustrated by Richard E. Hill

Side by Side Extra Book & eText 1

Pearson Education, 10 Bank Street, White Plains, NY 10606

Staff credits: The people who make up the *Side by Side Extra* team, representing content creation, design, manufacturing, marketing, multimedia, project management, publishing, rights management, and testing are Pietro Alongi, Allen Ascher, Rhea Banker, Elizabeth Barker, Lisa Bayrasli, Elizabeth Carlson, Jennifer Castro, Tracey Munz Cataldo, Diane Cipollone, Aerin Csigay, Victoria Denkus, Dave Dickey, Daniel Dwyer, Wanda España, Oliva Fernandez, Warren Fischbach, Pam Fishman, Nancy Flaggman, Patrice Fraccio, Irene Frankel, Aliza Greenblatt, Lester Holmes, Janet Johnston, Caroline Kasterine, Barry Katzen, Ray Keating, Renee Langan, Jaime Lieber, José Antonio Méndez, Julie Molnar, Alison Pei, Pamela Pia, Stuart Radcliffe, Jennifer Raspiller, Kriston Reinmuth, Mary Perrotta Rich, Tania Saiz-Sousa, Katherine Sullivan, Paula Van Ells, Kenneth Volcjak, and Wendy Wolf.

Contributing authors: Laura English, Megan Ernst, Meredith Westfall

Text composition: TSI Graphics, Inc.

Illustrations: Richard E. Hill

Photo credits: Page 25 pablocalvog/Fotolia; p. 26 (top left) Juice Images/Alamy, (top right) Kim Steele/ Blend Images/Getty Images, (bottom left) Image Source/Getty Images, (bottom right) mimagephotography/ Shutterstock; p. 54 (top) Hill Street Studios/Blend Images/Getty Images, (bottom) Monkey Business/Fotolia; p. 77 (left) Julie Campbell/Shutterstock, (middle) Ami Parikh/Shutterstock, (right) Greg Blomberg/Fotolia; p. 78 (top) John Warburton Lee/SuperStock, (middle top) jacky chapman/Alamy, (middle bottom) Zoriah/The Image Works, (bottom) Zefa RF/Alamy; p. 98 (top) CandyBox Images/Fotolia, (middle top) Robert Churchill/ iStockphoto/Getty Images, (middle bottom) camihesse/Fotolia, (bottom) Image Source/Getty Images; p. 115 WoodyStock/Alamy; p. 116 (top left) Gary Conner/Photodisc/Getty Images, (bottom left) Image Source/Getty Images, (middle) Pixel Embargo/Fotolia, (right) Steve Mason/Photodisc/Getty Images; p. 140 (top) A3528 Armin Weigel Deutsch Presse Agentur/Newscom, (middle) pressmaster/Fotolia, (bottom) IS2 from Image Source/Alamy; p. 165 (top) Philip Scalia/Alamy, (bottom left) Radharc Images/Alamy, (bottom right) Robert Landau/Alamy; P. 166 (top left) vannphoto/Fotolia, (top middle) Chris Howes/Wild Places Photography/ Alamy, (top right) ABW Photography/Purestock/SuperStock, (bottom left) Caro/Alamy, (bottom middle) Ariel Skelley/Blend Images/Getty Images, (bottom right) Patti McConville/Alamy.

The authors gratefully acknowledge the contribution of Tina Carver in the development of the original *Side by Side* program.

Side by Side Extra Book & eText 1: ISBN 13 – 978-0-13-245884-9; ISBN 10 – 0-13-245884-5
1 2 3 4 5 6 7 8 9 10–V082–22 21 20 19 18 17 16 15

Side by Side Extra Book & eText with Audio CD 1: ISBN 13 – 978-0-13-430672-8; ISBN 10 – 0-13-430672-4
1 2 3 4 5 6 7 8 9 10–V082–22 21 20 19 18 17 16 15

Side by Side Extra Book & eText International 1: ISBN 13 – 978-0-13-430651-3; ISBN 10 –0-13-430651-1
1 2 3 4 5 6 7 8 9 10–V082–22 21 20 19 18 17 16 15

Printed in the United States of America

CONTENTS

To Be: Introduction

- **Personal Information**
- **Meeting People**

VOCABULARY PREVIEW

① Aa Bb Cc Dd Ee Ff Gg
Hh Ii Jj Kk Ll Mm Nn
Oo Pp Qq Rr Ss Tt Uu
Vv Ww Xx Yy Zz

② 0 1 2 3 4 5 6 7 8 9 10

1. alphabet
2. numbers

235 Main Street

741-8906

3. name
4. address
5. telephone number
   phone number

What's Your Name?

* What's = What is
  235 = two thirty-five
  741-8906 = seven four one – eight nine "oh" six

Answer these questions.

1. What's your name?

   _____.

2. What's your address?

   _____.

3. What's your phone number?

   _____.

4. Where are you from?

   _____.

Now practice with other students in your class.

Interview a famous person. Make up addresses, phone numbers, and cities. Use your imagination! Practice with another student. Then present your role play to the class.

A. What's your name?

B. My name is _____.

A. _____ address?

B. _____.

A. _____ phone number?

B. _____.

A. Where are you from?

B. _____.

a famous actor

a famous actress

a famous athlete

the president*
of your country

How to Say It!

Meeting People

A. Hello. My name is *Peter Lewis*.

B. Hi. I'm *Nancy Lee*. Nice to meet you.

A. Nice to meet you, too.

Practice conversations with other students.

* president / prime minister / leader

WHAT'S YOUR NAME?

My name is David Carter. I'm American. I'm from San Francisco.

My name is Mrs. Grant. My phone number is 549-2376.

My name is Ms. Martinez. My telephone number is (213) 694-5555. My fax number is (213) 694-5557.

My name is Peter Black. My address is 378 Main Street, Waterville, Florida. My license number is 921DCG.

My name is Susan Miller. My apartment number is 4-B.

My name is Mr. Santini. My e-mail address is TeacherJoe@worldnet.com.*

My name is William Chen. My address is 294 River Street, Brooklyn, New York. My telephone number is 469-7750. My social security number is 044-35-9862.

* "TeacherJoe at worldnet-dot-com"

✔ READING *CHECK-UP*

MATCH

_____ 1. name   a. 549-2376

_____ 2. address   b. 4-B

_____ 3. phone number   c. TeacherJoe@worldnet.com

_____ 4. apartment number   d. William Chen

_____ 5. social security number   e. 378 Main Street

_____ 6. e-mail address   f. 044-35-9862

LISTENING

Listen and choose the correct answer.

1. a. Mary Black
    b. Mrs. Grant

2. a. 265 River Street
    b. 265 Main Street

3. a. 5-C
    b. 9-D

4. a. 295-4870
    b. 259-4087

5. a. 032-98-6175
    b. 032-89-6179

6. a. maryb@worldnet.com
    b. garyd@worldnet.com

INTERVIEW *Spelling Names*

Practice the conversation.

A. What's your last name?
B. *Kelly*.
A. How do you spell that?
B. *K-E-L-L-Y*.
A. What's your first name?
B. *Sarah*.
A. How do you spell that?
B. *S-A-R-A-H*.

Now interview students in your class.

	LAST NAME	FIRST NAME
1.		
2.		
3.		
4.		
5.		
6.		
7.		
8.		

PRONUNCIATION *Linked Sounds*

Listen. Then say it.

My name is Maria.

My address is 10 Main Street.

My apartment number is 3B.

Say it. Then listen.

My name is David.

My address is 9 River Street.

My phone number is 941-2238.

Write about yourself in your journal.

My name is _____.

My address is _____.

My phone number is _____.

I'm from _____.

GRAMMAR FOCUS

TO BE: AM/IS/ARE

am	I'm from Mexico City. (I am)
is	What's your name? (What is) My name is Maria.
are	Where are you from?

I'M/MY/YOU/YOUR

I'm My	I'm from San Francisco. My name is Maria.
you your	Where are you from? What's your name?

Choose the correct word.

1. My name (are   is) Carlos.
2. Where (are   is) you from?
3. I (are   am) from Los Angeles.
4. My phone number (are   is) 954-3376.
5. (I   I'm) from Miami.

Choose the correct word.

6. (I'm   My) address is 25 Center Street.
7. (I'm   My) from Chicago.
8. What's (you   your) social security number?
9. Where are (you   your) from?
10. Hello. (I'm   My) David Wong.

To Be + Location
Subject Pronouns

- **Classroom Objects**
- **Rooms in the Home**
- **Cities and Nationalities**
- **Places Around Town**

VOCABULARY PREVIEW

1. pen
2. pencil
3. book
4. desk
5. computer

6. bank
7. supermarket
8. post office
9. restaurant
10. library

11. living room
12. dining room
13. kitchen
14. bedroom
15. bathroom

1. pen	6. globe	10. clock	14. chair
2. book	7. map	11. bulletin board	15. ruler
3. pencil	8. board	12. computer	16. desk
4. notebook	9. wall	13. table	17. dictionary
5. bookshelf			

Where Is It?

| (Where is) Where's the book? | (It is) It's on the desk. |

  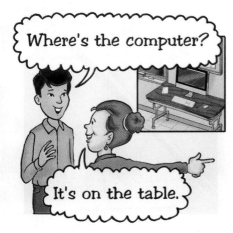

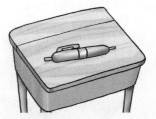

1. Where's the pen?

2. Where's the board?

3. Where's the globe?

4. Where's the ruler?

5. Where's the pencil?

6. Where's the clock?

7. Where's the notebook?

8. Where's the dictionary?

9. Where's the bulletin board?

Make a List!

Work with another student. Make a list of all the objects in your classroom. Present your list to the class. Who has the best list?

At Home

1. living room
2. dining room
3. kitchen

4. bedroom
5. bathroom
6. attic

7. yard
8. garage
9. basement

Where Are You?

am I	(I am) I'm
is { he / she / it } ?	(He is) He's / (She is) She's / (It is) It's } in the kitchen.
Where	
are { we / you / they }	(We are) We're / (You are) You're / (They are) They're

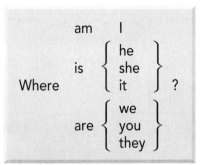

Where are you? — *I'm in the kitchen.*

Where are you? — **We're in the living room.**

Where are Mr. and Mrs. Jones? — **They're in the yard.**

1. Where are you?

2. Where are you?

3. Where are Jim and Pam?

4. Where are you?

5. Where are Mr. and Mrs. Park?

6. Where are you?

7. Where are you?

8. Where are you and Ben?

9. Where are Mr. and Mrs. Hernandez?

Where's Bob?

* Where's = Where is

1. Where's Tim?

2. Where's Rosa?

3. Where's the newspaper?

4. Where's Peggy?

5. Where's the telephone book?

6. Where's Harry?

7. Where's Ellen?

8. Where's Kevin?

9. Where's the cell phone?

READING

THE STUDENTS IN MY ENGLISH CLASS

The students in my English class are very interesting. Henry is Chinese. He's from Shanghai. Linda is Puerto Rican. She's from San Juan. Mr. and Mrs. Kim are Korean. They're from Seoul.

George is Greek. He's from Athens. Carla is Italian. She's from Rome. Mr. and Mrs. Sato are Japanese. They're from Tokyo. My friend Maria and I are Mexican. We're from Mexico City.

Yes, the students in my English class are very interesting. We're from many different countries . . . and we're friends.

✔ READING *CHECK-UP*

TRUE OR FALSE?

____ 1. Linda is Korean.

____ 2. George is Greek.

____ 3. Henry is from Mexico City.

____ 4. Mr. Kim is from Seoul.

____ 5. Carla is Chinese.

____ 6. The students in the class are from many countries.

How About You?

Tell about the students in YOUR English class. Where are they from?

How to Say It!

Greeting People

A. Hi. How are you?
B. Fine. And you?
A. Fine, thanks.

Practice conversations with other students.

Where Are They?

Ask and answer questions based on these pictures.

1. _____ Albert?

_____ .

2. _____ Carmen?

_____ .

3. _____ Walter and Mary?

_____ .

4. _____ you?

_____ .

5. _____ you?

_____ .

6. _____ Kate?

_____ .

7. _____ Mr. and Mrs. Lee?

_____ .

8. _____ monkey?

_____ .

9. _____ I?

_____ .

Now add people and places of your own.

10. _____ ?

_____ .

11. _____ ?

_____ .

12. _____ ?

_____ .

READING

George

Maria

SOCIAL
SECURITY

Mr. and Mrs. Sato

our English teacher

ALL THE STUDENTS IN MY ENGLISH CLASS ARE ABSENT TODAY

All the students in my English class are absent today. George is absent. He's in the hospital. Maria is absent. She's at the dentist. Mr. and Mrs. Sato are absent. They're at the social security office. Even our English teacher is absent. He's home in bed!

What a shame! Everybody in my English class is absent today. Everybody except me.

✔ **READING** *CHECK-UP*

WHAT'S THE ANSWER?

1. Where's George?
2. Where's Maria?
3. Where are Mr. and Mrs. Sato?
4. Where's the English teacher?

How About You?

Tell about YOUR English class:
Which students are in class today?
Which students are absent today?
Where are they?

LISTENING

WHAT'S THE WORD?

Listen and choose the correct answer.

1. a. bank   b. park
2. a. hospital   b. library
3. a. He's   b. She's
4. a. He's   b. She's
5. a. We're   b. They're
6. a. We're   b. They're

WHERE ARE THEY?

Listen and choose the correct place.

1. a. living room   b. dining room
2. a. bathroom   b. bedroom
3. a. garage   b. yard
4. a. bathroom   b. bedroom
5. a. kitchen   b. living room
6. a. bedroom   b. basement

PRONUNCIATION Reduced *and*

Mr. and Mrs.

Listen. Then say it.

Mr. and Mrs. Jones

Mr. and Mrs. Park

Jim and Pam

You and Ben

Say it. Then listen.

Mr. and Mrs. Lee

Mr. and Mrs. Miller

Walter and Mary

Jim and I

SIDE by SIDE JOURNAL

Draw a picture of your apartment or house. Label the rooms.

Project

Work with another student. Draw a picture of your classroom. Label all the objects.

GRAMMAR FOCUS

SUBJECT PRONOUNS
TO BE + LOCATION

Where	am	I?
	is	he? she? it?
	are	we? you? they?

(I am)	I'm	
(He is) (She is) (It is)	He's She's It's	in the kitchen.
(We are) (You are) (They are)	We're You're They're	

Choose the correct words.

1. A. Where (is are) Mrs. Chen?
   B. (He's She's) in the library.

2. A. Where (am are) you?
   B. (I'm It's) in the kitchen.

3. A. Where (am is) Mr. Grant?
   B. (She's He's) in the classroom.

4. A. Where (is are) the pen?
   B. (It's They're) on the desk.

5. A. Where (are am) Mr. and Mrs. Kim?
   B. (He's They're) in the restaurant.

6. A. Where (is are) you and John?
   B. (We're They're) in the park.

3

Present Continuous Tense

- **Everyday Activities**

1. eating	6. teaching	11. watching TV
2. drinking	7. singing	12. listening to music
3. cooking	8. sleeping	13. playing cards
4. reading	9. swimming	14. playing baseball
5. studying	10. planting	15. playing the piano

What Are You Doing?

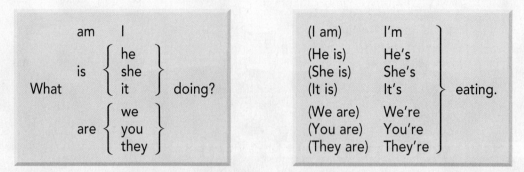

1. **A.** What are you doing?
   B. _____ reading the newspaper.

2. **A.** _____ Mr. and Mrs. Lane doing?
   B. _____ cooking dinner.

3. **A.** _____ you and Judy doing?
   B. _____ eating dinner.

4. **A.** _____ Rita doing?
   B. _____ studying English.

5. **A.** _____ Henry doing?
   B. _____ sleeping.

6. **A.** _____ Carol and Ken doing?
   B. _____ watching TV.

7. **A.** _____ Irene doing?
   B. _____ playing the piano.

8. **A.** What are YOU doing? _____
   B. I'm _____.

What's Everybody Doing?

A. Where's Walter?

B. He's in the kitchen.

A. What's he doing?

B. He's eating breakfast.

1. *Karen*
park
eating lunch

2. *Mr. and Mrs. Clark*
dining room
eating dinner

3. *you*
bedroom
playing the guitar

4. *you*
living room
playing cards

5. *Gary and Jane*
yard
playing baseball

6. *Miss Baker*
cafeteria
drinking milk

7. *you*
library
studying English

8. *Ms. Johnson*
classroom
teaching mathematics

9. *Marvin*
bathroom
singing

10. *Martha*
hospital
watching TV

11. *your friend*
park
listening to music

12.

How to Say It!

Checking Understanding

A. Where's *Walter*?
B. *He's* in the *kitchen*.
A. In the *kitchen*?
B. Yes.

Practice conversations with other students.

Action Game!

What am I doing?

You're playing the guitar.

Pantomime an everyday activity for the class. Ask students, "What am I doing?"

IN THE PARK

The Jones family is in the park today. The sun is shining, and the birds are singing. It's a beautiful day!

Mr. Jones is reading the newspaper. Mrs. Jones is listening to the radio. Sally and Patty Jones are studying. And Tommy Jones is playing the guitar.

The Jones family is very happy today. It's a beautiful day, and they're in the park.

AT HOME IN THE YARD

The Chen family is at home in the yard today. The sun is shining, and the birds are singing. It's a beautiful day!

Mr. Chen is planting flowers. Mrs. Chen is drinking lemonade and reading a book. Emily and Jason Chen are playing with the dog. And Jennifer Chen is sleeping.

The Chen family is very happy today. It's a beautiful day, and they're at home in the yard.

✔ READING CHECK-UP

TRUE OR FALSE?

_____ 1. The Jones family is at home in the yard today.

_____ 2. Mrs. Chen is planting flowers.

_____ 3. Patty Jones is studying.

_____ 4. Jason Chen is reading a book.

_____ 5. The Chen family is singing.

_____ 6. The Jones family and the Chen family are very happy today.

Q & A

Using this model, make questions and answers based on the stories on page 22.

A. *What's Mr. Jones doing?*
B. *He's reading the newspaper.*

LISTENING

Listen and choose the correct answer.

1. a. She's studying.
   b. I'm studying.

2. a. He's eating.
   b. She's eating.

3. a. He's watching TV.
   b. She's watching TV.

4. a. We're cooking dinner.
   b. They're cooking dinner.

5. a. We're planting flowers.
   b. They're planting flowers.

6. a. You're playing baseball.
   b. We're playing baseball.

IN YOUR OWN WORDS

FOR WRITING AND DISCUSSION

Mr. and Mrs. Martinez

Alex Martinez

Tina Martinez

Jimmy Martinez

AT THE BEACH

The Martinez family is at the beach today. Using this picture, tell a story about the Martinez family.

PRONUNCIATION Reduced *What are* & *Where are*

Listen. Then say it.

What are you doing?

What are Jim and Jane doing?

Where are Mary and Fred?

Where are you and Judy?

Say it. Then listen.

What are they doing?

What are Carol and Ken doing?

Where are Mr. and Mrs. Lane?

Where are you and Henry?

What are you doing now?
What are your friends doing?
Write about it in your journal.

GRAMMAR FOCUS

PRESENT CONTINUOUS TENSE

What	am	I	doing?
	is	he she it	
	are	we you they	

(I am)	I'm	eating.
(He is) (She is) (It is)	He's She's It's	
(We are) (You are) (They are)	We're You're They're	

Match the questions and answers.

____ **1.** What's Mr. Baker doing?

____ **2.** What are Susan and Jane doing?

____ **3.** What are you and Sam doing?

____ **4.** What's Ms. Garcia doing?

____ **5.** What are you doing?

____ **6.** What am I doing?

a. She's reading a book.

b. We're eating lunch.

c. He's cooking dinner.

d. You're playing the piano.

e. They're studying.

f. I'm watching TV.

Complete the sentences.

7. A. What _____ Mr. Yamamoto doing?

B. _____ sleeping.

8. A. What _____ Mr. and Mrs. Wu doing?

B. _____ eating breakfast.

9. A. What _____ I doing?

B. _____ swimming.

10. A. _____ are you and Carol doing?

B. _____ playing cards.

11. A. _____ _____ you doing?

B. _____ reading a book.

12. A. _____ _____ Ms. Lopez doing?

B. _____ listening to music.

BUILD YOUR VOCABULARY!

Playing Instruments, Sports, and Games

FACT FILE

Titles

Mr. is a title for a man.
Ms., Mrs., and Miss are titles for a woman.

Nicknames

My name is David.
My nickname is Dave.

COMMON NICKNAMES

Name	Nickname	Name	Nickname
James	Jim	Elizabeth	Liz, Betty
Peter	Pete	Jennifer	Jenny
Robert	Bob	Judith	Judy
Timothy	Tim	Katherine	Kathy, Kate
Thomas	Tom	Patricia	Patty
William	Bill	Susan	Sue

Global Exchange

SungHee: Hello. My name is Sung Hee. I'm Korean. I'm from Seoul. I'm a student. Right now I'm in my English class. I'm looking for a keypal in a different country.

DanielR: Hi, Sung Hee! My name is Daniel. My nickname is Danny. My last name is Rivera. I'm Mexican. I'm from Mexico City. I'm a student. Right now I'm at home. I'm at my computer, and I'm listening to music. I'm also looking for a keypal. Tell me about your school and your English class.

Send a message over the Internet. Tell about yourself.
Look for a keypal.

I'm playing _____ .

Instruments

 ■ the violin

 ■ the clarinet

 ■ the trumpet

Sports

 ■ soccer

 ■ tennis

 ■ basketball

Games

 ■ chess

 ■ checkers

 ■ tic tac toe

Greetings

Right now, all around the world, people are greeting each other in different ways.

They're shaking hands.

They're kissing.

They're bowing.

They're hugging.

How are people in your country greeting each other today?

LISTENING

You have seven messages!

You Have Seven Messages!

Messages

_c_ ❶	**a.**	Mrs. Lane 731–0248
___ ❷	**b.**	Linda Lee 969–0159
___ ❸	**c.**	Henry Drake 427–9168
___ ❹	**d.**	Dad
___ ❺	**e.**	Patty
___ ❻	**f.**	Jim 682–4630
___ ❼	**g.**	Kevin Carter 298–4577

What Are They Saying?

To Be: Short Answers
Possessive Adjectives

- **Everyday Activities**

VOCABULARY PREVIEW

1. brushing
2. cleaning
3. feeding
4. fixing
5. painting
6. reading
7. washing

I'm Fixing My Sink

I	my
he	his
she	her
it	its
we	our
you	your
they	their

Hi! What are you doing?

I'm fixing my sink.

What's Bob doing?

He's fixing his car.

What's Mary doing?

She's cleaning her room.

What are you doing?

We're cleaning our apartment.

What are your children doing?

They're doing their homework.

Are You Busy?

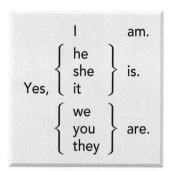

Yes, I am.
he
she   is.
it
we
you   are.
they

Are you busy?

Yes, I am.
I'm washing my hair.

1. Is Frank busy?
cleaning his apartment

2. Is Helen busy?
feeding her cat

3. Are you busy?
fixing our TV

4. Are Jim and Lisa busy?
painting their bedroom

5. Are you busy?
doing my homework

6. Is Richard busy?
washing his clothes

29

7. Are Ed and Ruth busy?
painting their garage

8. Is Timmy busy?
feeding his dog

9. Are you busy?
doing our exercises

10. Are you busy?
fixing my bicycle

11. Is Karen busy?
washing her car

12. Is Anwar busy?
cleaning his yard

13. Are your children busy?
brushing their teeth

14. Are you busy?
washing our windows

15. Is Wendy busy?
reading her e-mail

How to Say It!

Attracting Someone's Attention

A. Jane?
B. Yes?
A. What are you doing?
B. I'm *doing my exercises.*

Practice conversations with other students.

TALK ABOUT IT! *Where Are They, and What Are They Doing?*

Use these models to talk about the picture with other students in your class.

A. Where's *Mr. Molina*?

B. *He's* in the *park*.

A. What's *he* doing?

B. *He's listening to the radio.*

A. Where are *Mr. and Mrs. Sharp*?

B. They're in the *laundromat*.

A. What are they doing?

B. They're *washing their clothes.*

A BUSY DAY

Everybody at 159 River Street is very busy today. Mr. Price is cleaning his bedroom. Ms. Hunter is painting her bathroom. Ricky Gomez is feeding his cat. Mr. and Mrs. Wong are washing their clothes. Mrs. Martin is doing her exercises. And Judy and Larry Clark are fixing their car.

I'm busy, too. I'm washing my windows . . . and of course, I'm watching all my neighbors. It's a very busy day at 159 River Street.

✔ READING *CHECK-UP*

TRUE OR FALSE?

____ 1. Mr. Price is in his bedroom.

____ 2. Ricky is eating.

____ 3. Mr. and Mrs. Clark are in their apartment.

____ 4. Mrs. Martin is doing her exercises.

____ 5. Their address is 195 River Street.

Q & A

Using this model, make questions and answers based on the story.

    A. *What's Mr. Price* doing?
    B. *He's cleaning his bedroom.*

LISTENING

Listen and choose the correct answer.

1. a. The newspaper.
   b. Breakfast.

2. a. Her e-mail.
   b. Dinner.

3. a. The dining room.
   b. Soccer.

4. a. Their kitchen.
   b. Basketball.

5. a. TV.
   b. My clothes.

6. a. His neighbors.
   b. His windows.

IN YOUR OWN WORDS

FOR WRITING AND DISCUSSION

A BUSY DAY

Alex Molina

Jessica Harris

Mr. and Mrs. Chang

Mr. Sharp

MAIN STREET

320

Patty Williams

Mr. and Mrs. Hassan

Hector Lopez

Everybody at 320 Main Street is very busy today. Tell a story about them, using this picture and the story on page 32 as a guide.

PRONUNCIATION Deleted *h*

Listen. Then say it.

She's fixing her car.

She's cleaning her room.

He's feeding his dog.

He's washing his windows.

Say it. Then listen.

He's painting his apartment.

She's doing her homework.

He's brushing his teeth.

She's reading her e-mail.

Go to a place in your community—a park, a library, a supermarket, or someplace else. Look at the people. What are they doing? Write about it in your journal.

GRAMMAR FOCUS

TO BE: SHORT ANSWERS

	I	am.
Yes,	he she it	is.
	we you they	are.

POSSESSIVE ADJECTIVES

I'm He's She's It's We're You're They're	cleaning	my his her its our your their	room.

Match the questions and answers.

_____ **1.** Is Mr. Montero busy?

_____ **2.** Are Bob and Ellen busy?

_____ **3.** Is Mrs. Green busy?

_____ **4.** Are you and Rita busy?

_____ **5.** Are you busy?

a. Yes, they are.

b. Yes, I am.

c. Yes, we are.

d. Yes, he is.

e. Yes, she is.

Complete the sentences.

6. I'm cleaning _____ apartment.

7. Mr. Sato is painting _____ garage.

8. Mrs. Miller is feeding _____ cat.

9. David and I are washing _____ windows.

10. My children are doing _____ homework.

11. Are you brushing _____ teeth?

To Be: Yes/No Questions
Short Answers

Adjectives
Possessive Nouns

- **Describing People and Things**
- **Weather**

VOCABULARY PREVIEW

1. tall – short	**5.** married – single	**9.** noisy/loud – quiet
2. young – old	**6.** handsome – ugly	**10.** expensive – cheap
3. heavy/fat – thin	**7.** beautiful/pretty – ugly	**11.** easy – difficult
4. new – old	**8.** large/big – small/little	**12.** rich – poor

Tall or Short?

(I am)	I'm
(He is)	He's
(She is)	She's
(It is)	It's
(We are)	We're
(You are)	You're
(They are)	They're

tall.

Bob   Bill

A. Is Bob tall or short?

B. He's tall.

A. Is Bill tall or short?

B. He's short.

Ask and answer these questions.

Kate   Peggy

1. Is Kate young or old?
2. Is Peggy young or old?

Howard   Mike

3. Is Howard heavy or thin?
4. Is Mike fat or thin?

Howard's car   Mike's car

5. Is Howard's car new or old?
6. Is Mike's car new or old?

Gloria   Jennifer

7. Is Gloria married or single?
8. Is Jennifer married or single?

9. Is Robert handsome or ugly?

10. Is Captain Crook handsome or ugly?

11. Is Vanessa beautiful or ugly?

12. Is Hilda pretty or ugly?

13. Is Robert's house large or small?

14. Is George's apartment big or little?

15. Are Kate's neighbors noisy or quiet?

16. Are Peggy's neighbors loud or quiet?

17. Is the food at the Plaza Restaurant expensive or cheap?

18. Is the food at Burger Town expensive or cheap?

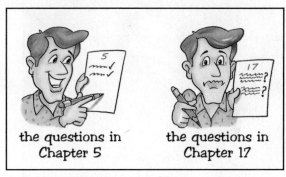

19. Are the questions in Chapter 5 easy or difficult?

20. Are the questions in Chapter 17 easy or difficult?

21. Is Marvin rich or poor?

22. Is Larry rich or poor?

Now ask and answer your own questions.

37

Tell Me About . . .

Am	I			
Is	{	he she it	tall?	
Are	{	we you they		

Yes,	I	am.
	he she it	is.
	we you they	are.

No,	I'm	not.
	he she it	isn't.
	we you they	aren't.

Are you married?

No, I'm not. I'm single.

Tell me about your new car. Is it large?

No, it isn't. It's small.

Tell me about your new neighbors. Are they quiet?

No, they aren't. They're noisy.

1. **A.** Tell me about your computer.
   _____ new?

   B. No, _____. _____.

2. **A.** Tell me about your new boss.
   _____ young?

   B. No, _____. _____.

3. **A.** Tell me about your neighbors.

_____ noisy?

B. No, _____. _____.

4. **A.** Tell me about the Plaza Restaurant.

_____ cheap?

B. No, _____. _____.

5. **A.** Tell me about your brother.

_____ tall?

B. No, _____. _____.

6. **A.** Tell me about your sister.

_____ single?

B. No, _____. _____.

7. **A.** Tell me about Nancy's cat.

_____ pretty?

B. No, _____. _____.

8. **A.** Tell me about Ron and Betty's dog.

_____ little?

B. No, _____. _____.

9. **A.** Tell me about the questions in your English book.

_____ difficult?

B. No, _____. _____.

10. **A.** Tell me about Santa Claus.

_____ thin?

B. No, _____. _____.

How's the Weather Today?

How's the weather today in YOUR city?

How to Say It!

Calling Someone You Know on the Telephone

A. Hello.
B. Hello. Is this *Julie*?
A. Yes, it is.
B. Hi, *Julie*. This is *Anna*.
A. Hi, *Anna*. . . .

Practice conversations with other students.

The Weather Is Terrible Here!

A. Hi, Jack. This is Jim. I'm calling from Miami.

B. From Miami? What are you doing in Miami?

A. I'm on vacation.

B. How's the weather in Miami? Is it sunny?

A. No, it isn't. It's raining.

B. Is it hot?

A. No, it isn't. It's cold.

B. Are you having a good time?

A. No, I'm not. I'm having a TERRIBLE time.
The weather is TERRIBLE here!

B. I'm sorry to hear that.

A. Hi, _____. This is _____. I'm calling from _____.

B. From _____? What are you doing in _____?

A. I'm on vacation.

B. How's the weather in _____? Is it _____?

A. No, it isn't. It's _____.

B. Is it _____?

A. No, it isn't. It's _____.

B. Are you having a good time?

A. No, I'm not. I'm having a TERRIBLE time. The weather is TERRIBLE here!

B. I'm sorry to hear that.

1. *British Columbia*
   cool?
   snowing?

2. *Tahiti*
   hot?
   sunny?

You're on vacation, and the weather is terrible! Call a student in your class. Use the conversation above as a guide.

41

DEAR MOTHER

Royal Sludge Hotel

Dear Mother,

I'm writing from our hotel at Sludge Beach. Ralph and I are on vacation with the children for a few days. We're happy to be here, but to tell the truth, we're having a few problems.

The weather isn't very good. In fact, it's cold and cloudy. Right now I'm looking out the window, and it's raining cats and dogs.

The children aren't very happy. In fact, they're bored and they're having a terrible time. Right now they're sitting on the bed, playing tic tac toe and watching TV.

The restaurants here are expensive, and the food isn't very good. In fact, Ralph is at a clinic right now. He's having problems with his stomach.

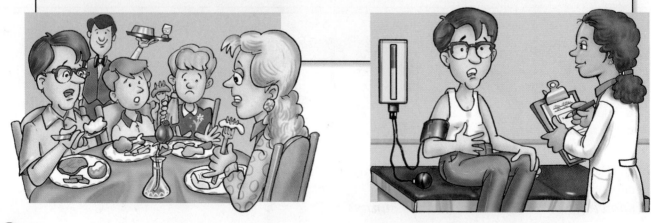

All the other hotels here are beautiful and new. Our hotel is ugly, and it's very, very old. In fact, right now a repairperson is fixing the bathroom sink.

So, Mother, we're having a few problems here at Sludge Beach, but we're happy. We're happy to be on vacation, and we're happy to be together.

See you soon.

Love,

Ethel

✓ READING *CHECK-UP*

TRUE OR FALSE?

____ 1. The weather is beautiful.

____ 2. The children are happy.

____ 3. The children are watching TV.

____ 4. The restaurants are cheap.

____ 5. Ralph is at the hotel right now.

____ 6. Their hotel is old.

____ 7. A repairperson is fixing the window.

____ 8. Ethel is watching the cats and dogs.

LISTENING

WHAT'S THE ANSWER?

Listen and choose the correct answer.

1. a. It's large.   b. It's heavy.
2. a. It's married.   b. It's beautiful.
3. a. They're quiet.   b. They're sunny.
4. a. It's young.   b. It's warm.
5. a. It's small.   b. It's easy.
6. a. It's good.   b. It's raining.

TRUE OR FALSE?

Listen to the conversation. Then answer *True* or *False*.

1. Louise is calling Betty.
2. The weather is hot and sunny.
3. The hotel is old.
4. The food is very good.
5. Louise is watching TV.

Listen. Then say it.

Is Bob tall or short?

Is Kate young or old?

Are they noisy or quiet?

Is it hot or cold?

Say it. Then listen.

Is the car new or old?

Are you married or single?

Is it sunny or cloudy?

Are they large or small?

SIDE by SIDE JOURNAL

How's the weather today?
What are you doing now?
Write a letter to a friend
and tell about it.

GRAMMAR FOCUS

To Be: Yes / No Questions

Am	I	
Is	he she it	tall?
Are	we you they	

To Be: Short Answers

	I	am.
Yes,	he she it	is.
	we you they	are.

	I'm	not.
No,	he she it	isn't.
	we you they	aren't.

Complete the sentences.

1. A. _____ he tall?
   B. Yes, _____ _____.

2. A. _____ they new?
   B. Yes, _____ _____.

3. A. _____ she short?
   B. No, _____ _____.

4. A. _____ you and Roberto busy?
   B. Yes, _____ _____.

5. A. _____ your homework difficult?
   B. No, _____ _____.

6. A. _____ your neighbors quiet?
   B. No, _____ _____.

7. A. _____ you single?
   B. Yes, _____ _____.

8. A. _____ it raining?
   B. Yes, _____ _____.

9. A. _____ you heavy?
   B. No, _____ _____.

10. A. _____ you and Alicia busy?
    B. No, _____ _____.

11. A. _____ your sister married?
    B. Yes, _____ _____.

12. A. _____ Mr. Lee in Miami?
    B. No, _____ _____.

6

To Be: Review
Present Continuous Tense: Review
Prepositions of Location

- Family Members
- Describing Activities and Events

VOCABULARY PREVIEW

1. wife	**children**	**grandparents**	**grandchildren**	13. aunt
2. husband	5. daughter	9. grandmother	11. granddaughter	14. uncle
	6. son	10. grandfather	12. grandson	15. niece
parents	7. sister			16. nephew
3. mother	8. brother			17. cousin
4. father				

My Favorite Photographs

A. Who is he?

B. He's my father.

A. What's his name?

B. His name is Paul.

A. Where is he?

B. He's in Paris.

A. What's he doing?

B. He's standing in front of the Eiffel Tower.

Using these questions, talk about the following photographs.

Who is he?	Who is she?	Who are they?
What's his name?	What's her name?	What are their names?
Where is he?	Where is she?	Where are they?
What's he doing?	What's she doing?	What are they doing?

1. *my mother*
   in the park
   riding her bicycle

2. *my parents*
   in the dining room
   having dinner

3. *my son*
at the beach
swimming

4. *my daughter*
in front of our house
washing her car

5. *my wife*
in the yard
planting flowers

6. *my husband*
in our living room
sleeping on the sofa

7. *my sister and brother*
in the kitchen
baking a cake

8. *my grandmother and grandfather*
at my wedding
crying

9. *my aunt and uncle*
in Washington, D.C.
standing in front of the White House

10. *my cousin*
in front of his apartment building
skateboarding

11. *my niece*
at school
acting in a play

12. *my nephew*
in his bedroom
sitting on his bed and playing the guitar

13. *my friend*
in his apartment
playing a game on his computer

14. *my friends*
at my birthday party
singing and dancing

ON YOUR OWN   *Your Favorite Photographs*

This is a photograph of my sister and me. My sister's name is Amanda. We're in the park. Amanda is feeding the birds, and I'm sitting on a bench and listening to music.

Bring in your favorite photographs to class. Talk about them with other students. Ask the other students about *their* favorite photographs.

ARTHUR IS VERY ANGRY

It's late at night. Arthur is sitting on his bed, and he's looking at his clock. His neighbors are making a lot of noise, and Arthur is VERY angry.

The people in Apartment 2 are dancing. The man in Apartment 3 is vacuuming his rug. The woman in Apartment 4 is playing the drums. The teenagers in Apartment 5 are listening to loud music. The dog in Apartment 6 is barking. And the people in Apartment 7 are having a big argument.

It's very late, and Arthur is tired and angry. What a terrible night!

✔ READING CHECK-UP

Q & A

Using this model, make questions and answers based on the story.

A. *What's the man in Apartment 3 doing?*
B. *He's vacuuming his rugs.*

CHOOSE

1. Arthur's neighbors are _____.
   a. noisy
   b. angry

2. The man in Apartment 3 is _____.
   a. painting
   b. cleaning

3. The people in Apartment 5 are _____.
   a. young
   b. old

4. The dog in Apartment 6 isn't _____.
   a. sleeping
   b. making noise

5. The woman in Apartment 4 is _____.
   a. playing cards
   b. playing music

6. Arthur isn't very _____.
   a. happy
   b. tired

TOM'S WEDDING DAY

Today is a very special day. It's my wedding day, and all my family and friends are here. Everybody is having a wonderful time.

My wife, Jane, is standing in front of the fireplace. She's wearing a beautiful white wedding gown. Uncle Harry is taking her photograph, and Aunt Emma is crying. (She's very sentimental.)

The band is playing my favorite popular music. My mother is dancing with Jane's father, and Jane's mother is dancing with my father.

My sister and Jane's brother are standing in the yard and eating wedding cake. Our grandparents are sitting in the corner and talking about "the good old days."

Everybody is having a good time. People are singing, dancing, and laughing, and our families are getting to know each other. It's a very special day.

✔ **READING** *CHECK-UP*

WHAT'S THE ANSWER?

1. Where is Jane standing?
2. What's she wearing?
3. What's Uncle Harry doing?
4. What's Aunt Emma doing?
5. What's Tom's mother doing?
6. What are their grandparents doing?

LISTENING

QUIET OR NOISY?

Listen to the sentence. Are the people quiet or noisy?

1. a. quiet   b. noisy
2. a. quiet   b. noisy
3. a. quiet   b. noisy
4. a. quiet   b. noisy
5. a. quiet   b. noisy
6. a. quiet   b. noisy

WHAT DO YOU HEAR?

Listen to the sound. What do you hear? Choose the correct answer.

1. a. They're studying.   b. They're singing.
2. a. He's crying.   b. He's doing his exercises.
3. a. She's vacuuming.   b. She's washing her clothes.
4. a. They're barking.   b. They're laughing.
5. a. She's playing the piano.   b. She's playing the drums.

IN YOUR OWN WORDS

FOR WRITING AND DISCUSSION

JESSICA'S BIRTHDAY PARTY

Today is a very special day. It's Jessica's birthday party, and all her family and friends are there. Using this picture, tell a story about her party.

How to Say It!

Introducing People

A. I'd like to introduce *my brother*.
B. Nice to meet you.
C. Nice to meet you, too.

Practice conversations with other students.

PRONUNCIATION *Stressed and Unstressed Words*

Listen. Then say it.

He's pláying the guitár.

She's ácting in a pláy.

She's ríding her bícycle.

He's sléeping on the sófa.

Say it. Then listen.

We're báking a cáke.

They're sítting in the yárd.

He's wáshing his cár.

She's sítting on her béd.

SIDE by **SIDE** **JOURNAL**

Write in your journal about your favorite photograph.

This is a photograph of _____ .

In this photograph, _____

It's my favorite photograph because _____ .

GRAMMAR FOCUS

TO BE

Who is	he? she?
Who are	they?

He's my father. She's my wife.
They're my parents.

PRESENT CONTINUOUS TENSE

What's	he she	doing?
What are	they	doing?

He's She's	sleeping.
They're	swimming.

PREPOSITIONS OF LOCATION

She's **in** the park.	He's sitting **on** his bed.
He's **at** the beach.	We're **in front of** our house.

Complete the sentences.

1. A. Who _____ he?
   B. _____ my brother.
2. A. Who _____ they?
   B. _____ my grandparents.
3. A. Who is _____?
   B. _____ my daughter.
4. A. Who _____ _____?
   B. He's my son.

5. A. What's she _____?
   B. _____ baking.
6. A. What _____ they doing?
   B. _____ dancing.
7. A. _____ he doing?
   B. _____ vacuuming.
8. A. What's _____ _____?
   B. She's having dinner.

9. We're reading _____ the living room.
10. He's sleeping _____ the sofa.
11. I'm standing _____ _____ _____ my car.
12. My friends are crying _____ my wedding.

SIDE by SIDE Gazette

Volume 1   Number 2

A Family Tree

Betty and Henry Wilson's family tree is very large

A family tree is a diagram of the people in a family. This is the Wilson family tree. All the members of the Wilson family are on this family tree—parents, children, grandparents, grandchildren, aunts, uncles, cousins, nieces, and nephews.

Betty and Henry are the parents of Sally, Linda, and Tom. Linda is single. Sally is married. Her husband's name is Jack. Sally and Jack are the parents of Jimmy and Sarah. Jimmy is their son, and Sarah is their daughter.

Tom is also married. His wife's name is Patty. Patty and Tom are the parents of Julie and Kevin. Julie is their daughter, and Kevin is their son.

Jimmy, Sarah, Julie, and Kevin are cousins. They are also the grandchildren of Betty and Henry. (Betty and Henry are their grandparents.)

Jack is Julie and Kevin's uncle. Sally is their aunt. Tom is Jimmy and Sarah's uncle. Patty is their aunt. Linda is also the aunt of Jimmy, Sarah, Julie, and Kevin.

Jimmy is the nephew of Linda, Patty, and Tom. Sarah is their niece. Julie is the niece of Sally, Jack, and Linda. Kevin is their nephew.

Draw your family tree. Then write about it.

BUILD YOUR VOCABULARY!

Classroom Activities

I'm _____ .

■ reading

■ writing

■ raising my hand

■ opening my book

■ closing my book

■ erasing the board

■ using a calculator

Today's Weather

_d_ **1** hot   **a.** Atlanta

____ **2** snowing   **b.** Chicago

____ **3** warm and sunny   **c.** Toronto

____ **4** cool and sunny   **d.** Honolulu

____ **5** cold and cloudy   **e.** Los Angeles

AROUND THE WORLD

Extended and Nuclear Families

This is an **extended family.** The grandparents, parents, and children are all together in one apartment. An uncle, an aunt, and two cousins are in another apartment in the same building. Extended families are very common around the world.

This is a **nuclear family.** Only the mother, father, and children are in this home. The grandparents, aunts, uncles, and cousins are in different homes. Nuclear families are very common in many countries.

Is your family a nuclear family or an extended family? Which type of family is common in your country? In your opinion, what are some good things and bad things about these different types of families?

Global Exchange

Ken425: It's a beautiful day in our city today. It's warm and sunny. The people in my family are very busy. My brother and sister are cleaning our apartment. My mother is washing the windows, and my father is fixing the bathroom sink. I'm cooking dinner for my family. How about you? What's the weather today? What are you doing? What are other people in your family doing?

Send a message to a keypal. Tell about the weather, and tell about what you and others are doing today.

FACT FILE

Family Relationships

wife's mother husband's mother	=	mother-in-law
wife's father husband's father	=	father-in-law
son's wife	=	daughter-in-law
daughter's husband	=	son-in-law
wife's sister husband's sister	=	sister-in-law
wife's brother husband's brother	=	brother-in-law

What Are They Saying?

Prepositions
There Is/There Are
Singular/Plural: Introduction

- Places Around Town
- Locating Places
- Describing Neighborhoods
- Describing Apartments

VOCABULARY PREVIEW

1. bakery	6. clinic	11. hotel
2. barber shop	7. department store	12. laundromat
3. book store	8. drug store	13. school
4. bus station	9. hair salon	14. train station
5. cafeteria	10. health club	15. video store

Where's the Restaurant?

A. Where's the restaurant?
B. It's **next to** the bank.

A. Where's the school?
B. It's **between** the library and the park.

A. Where's the supermarket?
B. It's **across from** the movie theater.

A. Where's the post office?
B. It's **around the corner from** the hospital.

1. Where's the bank?

3. Where's the restaurant?

5. Where's the hotel?

7. Where's the clinic?

2. Where's the post office?

4. Where's the hospital?

6. Where's the gas station?

8. Where's the bakery?

Is There a Laundromat in This Neighborhood?

| There's (There is) a bank on Main Street. |
| Is there a bank on Main Street? |

A. Excuse me. Is there a laundromat in this neighborhood?

B. Yes. There's a laundromat on Main Street, next to the supermarket.

1. *drug store?*

2. *clinic?*

3. *department store?*

4. *hair salon?*

5. *book store?*

6. *post office?*

How to Say It!

Expressing Gratitude

A. Thank you. / Thanks.
B. You're welcome.

Practice some conversations on this page again.
Express gratitude at the end of each conversation.

Is there . . . ?

Yes, there is.
No, there isn't.

Is there a restaurant in your neighborhood?

No, there isn't.

Is there a cafeteria in your neighborhood?

Yes, there is.

Where is it?

It's on Central Avenue, across from the bank.

Draw a simple map of your neighborhood. With another student, ask and answer questions about your neighborhoods.

Some places you can talk about:

bakery	clinic	hospital	post office
bank	department store	hotel	restaurant
barber shop	drug store	laundromat	school
book store	fire station	library	supermarket
bus station	gas station	movie theater	train station
cafeteria	hair salon	park	video store
church	health club	police station	

Is There a Stove in the Kitchen?

A. Is there a stove in the kitchen?

B. Yes, there is. There's a very nice stove in the kitchen.

A. Oh, good.

A. Is there a refrigerator in the kitchen?

B. No, there isn't.

A. Oh, I see.

1. *a window in the kitchen?*
Yes, . . .

2. *a fire escape?*
No, . . .

3. *a closet in the bedroom?*
Yes, . . .

4. *an elevator* in the building?*
No, . . .

5. *an air conditioner* in the bedroom?*
Yes, . . .

6. *a superintendent in the building?*
No, . . .

7. *a bus stop near the building?*
No, . . .

8. *a jacuzzi in the bathroom?*
Yes, . . .

* **a** stove   **an** elevator
   a closet   **an** air conditioner

How Many Bedrooms Are There in the Apartment?

How many windows **are there** in the bedroom?	**There's** one window in the bedroom. **There are** two windows in the bedroom.

A. Tell me, how many bedrooms are there in the apartment?

B. There are two bedrooms in the apartment.

A. Two bedrooms?

B. Yes. That's right.

1. *floors*
   building

2. *windows*
   living room

3. *closets*
   apartment

4. *apartments*
   building

5. *washing machines*
   basement

6. *bathrooms*
   apartment

* two and a half

60

An Apartment Building

ROLE PLAY *Looking for an Apartment*

| Is there a window?
Yes, there is. / No, there isn't. | Are there any windows?
Yes, there are. / No, there aren't. |

You're looking for a new apartment. Practice with another student. Ask questions about the apartment on page 61.

Ask the landlord:

1. a stove in the kitchen?
2. a refrigerator in the kitchen?
3. a superintendent in the building?
4. an elevator in the building?
5. a fire escape?
6. a satellite dish on the roof?
7. a mailbox near the building?
8. a bus stop near the building?

Ask a tenant in the building:

9. children in the building?
10. cats in the building?
11. mice in the basement?
12. cockroaches in the building?
13. broken windows in the building?
14. holes in the walls?
15. washing machines in the basement?

Ask the landlord:

16. rooms—in the apartment?
17. floors—in the building?
18. closets—in the bedroom?
19. windows—in the living room?

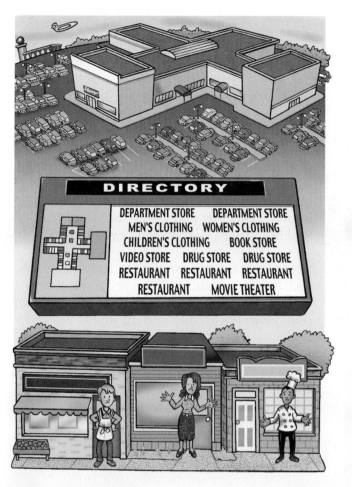

THE NEW SHOPPING MALL

Everybody in Brewster is talking about the city's new shopping mall. The mall is outside the city, next to the Brewster airport. There are more than one hundred stores in the mall.

There are two big department stores. There are many clothing stores for men, women, and children. There's a book store, and there's a video store. There are two drug stores, and there are four restaurants. There's even a large movie theater.

Almost all the people in Brewster are happy that their city's new shopping mall is now open. But some people aren't happy. The owners of the small stores in the old center of town are very upset. They're upset because many people aren't shopping in the stores in the center of town. They're shopping at the new mall.

✔ READING CHECK-UP

CHOOSE

1. Everybody in Brewster is _____.
   a. at the airport
   b. outside the city
   c. talking about the mall

2. In the mall, there are _____.
   a. two video stores
   b. two drug stores
   c. two restaurants

3. In the mall, there are _____.
   a. book stores and cafeterias
   b. restaurants and drug stores
   c. clothing stores and video stores

4. The store owners in the center of town are upset because _____.
   a. people aren't shopping in their stores
   b. people aren't shopping at the mall
   c. they're very old

How About You?

Is there a shopping mall in your city or town?
Are there small stores in your city or town?
Tell about stores where you live.

AMY'S APARTMENT BUILDING

Amy's apartment building is in the center of town. Amy is very happy there because the building is in a very convenient place.

Across from the building, there's a bank, a post office, and a restaurant. Next to the building, there's a drug store and a laundromat. Around the corner from the building, there are two supermarkets.

There's a lot of noise near Amy's apartment building. There are a lot of cars on the street, and there are a lot of people on the sidewalks all day and all night.

However, Amy isn't very upset about the noise in her neighborhood. Her building is in the center of town. It's a very busy place, but it's a convenient place to live.

 ## READING *CHECK-UP*

WHAT'S THE ANSWER?

1. Where is Amy's apartment building?
2. What's across from her building?
3. Is there a laundromat near her building?
4. Why is there a lot of noise near Amy's building?
5. Why is Amy happy there?

TRUE OR FALSE?

1. Amy's apartment is in a convenient place.
2. There's a drug store around the corner from her building.
3. There are two supermarkets in her neighborhood.
4. There are a lot of cars on the sidewalk.
5. The center of town is very noisy.

How About You?

Tell about YOUR neighborhood.
Is it convenient? Is it very busy?
Is it noisy or quiet?

IN YOUR OWN WORDS

FOR WRITING AND DISCUSSION

EDWARD'S APARTMENT BUILDING

Edward's apartment building is in the center of town. Edward is very happy there because the building is in a very convenient place. Using this picture, tell about Edward's neighborhood.

LISTENING

WHAT PLACES DO YOU HEAR?

Listen and choose the correct places.

Example: (a.) supermarket   b. school   (c.) video store

1. a. park   b. bank   c. laundromat
2. a. fire station   b. police station   c. gas station
3. a. school   b. department store   c. clothing store
4. a. bank   b. drug store   c. book store
5. a. hotel   b. hair salon   c. hospital

TRUE OR FALSE?

Listen to the conversation. Then answer *True* or *False*.

1. There are four rooms in the apartment.
2. There are two closets in the bedroom.
3. There are four windows in the kitchen.
4. There's a superintendent in the building.
5. There are three washing machines.
6. There's an elevator in the building.

Listen. Then say it.

Two bedrooms?

Five closets?

Next to the bank?

On Main Street?

Say it. Then listen.

Three windows?

Twenty floors?

Across from the clinic?

On Central Avenue?

In your journal, write about your apartment building or home. Tell about the building and the neighborhood.

GRAMMAR FOCUS

THERE IS/THERE ARE

There's one window in the bedroom.

Is there a laundromat in this neighborhood?

    Yes, **there is.**
    No, **there isn't.**

There are two windows in the bedroom.

Are there any children in the building?

    Yes, **there are.**
    No, **there aren't.**

SINGULAR/PLURAL: INTRODUCTION

There's one bedroom in the apartment.
There are two bedrooms in the apartment.

PREPOSITIONS

It's **next to** the bank.
It's **across from** the movie theater.
It's **between** the library and the park.
It's **around the corner from** the hospital.

Complete the sentences.

1. A. _____ there a clinic in this neighborhood?
   B. Yes, _____ _____.

2. A. _____ there cats in the building?
   B. Yes, _____ _____.

3. A. Is _____ a stove in the kitchen?
   B. No, _____ _____.

4. A. Are _____ mice in the basement?
   B. No, _____ _____.

5. A. How many rooms _____ there in the apartment?
   B. _____ _____ four rooms.

6. A. How many closets are _____ in the bedroom?
   B. _____ one closet in the bedroom.

7. The hospital is _____ the corner from the park.
8. The restaurant is _____ to the post office.
9. The hotel is _____ the bakery and the bank.
10. The gas station is across _____ the library.
11. The drug store is next _____ the laundromat.

Singular/Plural
Adjectives
This/That/These/Those

- **Clothing**
- **Colors**
- **Shopping for Clothing**

VOCABULARY PREVIEW

1. shirt	6. jacket	11. pants
2. coat	7. suit	12. jeans
3. dress	8. tie	13. pajamas
4. skirt	9. belt	14. shoes
5. blouse	10. sweater	15. socks

Clothing

1. shirt	**8.** earring	**15.** hat	**21.** suit
2. tie	**9.** necklace	**16.** coat	**22.** watch
3. jacket	**10.** blouse	**17.** glove	**23.** umbrella
4. belt	**11.** bracelet	**18.** purse/	**24.** sweater
5. pants	**12.** skirt	pocketbook	**25.** mitten
6. sock	**13.** briefcase	**19.** dress	**26.** jeans
7. shoe	**14.** stocking	**20.** glasses	**27.** boot

Shirts Are Over There

SINGULAR/PLURAL*

a shirt – shirts
a coat – coats
a hat – hats
a belt – belts

a tie – ties
an umbrella – umbrellas
a sweater – sweaters

a dress – dresses
a watch – watches
a blouse – blouses
a necklace – necklaces

A. Excuse me.
I'm looking for **a shirt**.

B. **Shirts** are over there.

A. Thanks.

A. Excuse me.
I'm looking for **a tie**.

B. **Ties** are over there.

A. Thanks.

A. Excuse me.
I'm looking for **a dress**.

B. **Dresses** are over there.

A. Thanks.

1.

2.

3.

4.

5.

6.

7.

8.

Put these words in the correct column.

| boots | briefcases | earrings | glasses | gloves | pants | purses | shoes | socks |

 S

boots

_____

_____

Z

_____

_____

_____

IZ

_____

_____

_____

* Some irregular plurals you know are:

| a man – men | a child – children | a tooth – teeth |
| a woman – women | a person – people | a mouse – mice |

I'm Looking for a Jacket

COLORS

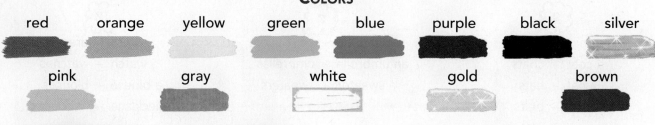

red   orange   yellow   green   blue   purple   black   silver

pink   gray   white   gold   brown

A. May I help you?

B. Yes, please. I'm looking for a jacket.

A. Here's a nice jacket.

B. But this is a PURPLE jacket!

A. That's okay. Purple jackets are very POPULAR this year.

A. May I help you?

B. Yes, please. I'm looking for a _____.

A. Here's a nice _____.

B. But this is a _____ _____!

A. That's okay. _____ _____s are very POPULAR this year.

1. *red*

2. *white*

3. *pink*

4. *orange*

5. *yellow*

6. *green and purple*

7. *striped*

8. *polka dot*

I'm Looking for a Pair of Gloves

pair of shoes/socks . . .

A. Can I help you?

B. Yes, please. I'm looking for a pair of gloves.

A. Here's a nice pair of gloves.

B. But these are GREEN gloves!

A. That's okay. Green gloves are very POPULAR this year.

A. Can I help you?

B. Yes, please. I'm looking for a pair of _____.

A. Here's a nice pair of _____.

B. But these are _____ _____s!

A. That's okay. _____ _____s are very POPULAR this year.

1. *yellow*

2. *blue*

3. *pink*

4. *orange*

5. *striped*

6. *green*

7. *red, white, and blue*

8. *polka dot*

How About You?

What are you wearing today?

What are the students in your class wearing today?

What's your favorite color?

NOTHING TO WEAR

Fred is upset this morning. He's looking for something to wear to work, but there's nothing in his closet.

He's looking for a clean shirt, but all his shirts are dirty. He's looking for a sports jacket, but all his sports jackets are at the dry cleaner's. He's looking for a pair of pants, but all the pants in his closet are ripped. And he's looking for a pair of socks, but all his socks are on the clothesline, and it's raining!

Fred is having a difficult time this morning. He's getting dressed for work, but his closet is empty, and there's nothing to wear.

✔ READING *CHECK-UP*

CHOOSE

1. Fred's closet is _____.
   a. upset
   b. empty

2. Fred is _____.
   a. at home
   b. at work

3. Fred's shirts are _____.
   a. dirty
   b. clean

4. He's looking for a pair of _____.
   a. jackets
   b. pants

5. The weather is _____.
   a. not very good
   b. beautiful

6. Fred is upset because _____.
   a. he's getting dressed
   b. there's nothing to wear

WHICH WORD DOESN'T BELONG?

Example:	a. socks	b. stockings	ⓒ jeans	d. shoes
1.	a. sweater	b. jacket	c. briefcase	d. coat
2.	a. necklace	b. belt	c. bracelet	d. earrings
3.	a. blouse	b. skirt	c. dress	d. tie
4.	a. clean	b. green	c. gray	d. blue
5.	a. pants	b. shoes	c. earrings	d. blouse

Excuse Me. I Think That's My Jacket.

This/That is	These/Those are

1. *hat* 2. *boots* 3. *coat* 4. *pen*

      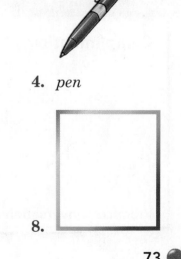

5. *pencils* 6. *umbrella* 7. *sunglasses* 8.

Lost and Found

A. Is this your umbrella?

B. No, it isn't.

A. Are you sure?

B. Yes. THAT umbrella is BROWN, and MY umbrella is BLACK.

A. Are these your boots?

B. No, they aren't.

A. Are you sure?

B. Yes. THOSE boots are DIRTY, and MY boots are CLEAN.

Make up conversations, using colors and other adjectives you know.

1. *watch*

2. *gloves*

3. *briefcase*

4. *mittens*

5. _____

How to Say It!

Complimenting

A. That's a very nice *hat*!
B. Thank you.

A. Those are very nice *boots*!
B. Thank you.

Practice conversations with other students.

74

READING

HOLIDAY SHOPPING

Mrs. Miller is doing her holiday shopping. She's looking for gifts for her family, but she's having a lot of trouble.

She's looking for a brown umbrella for her son, but all the umbrellas are black. She's looking for a gray raincoat for her daughter, but all the raincoats are yellow. She's looking for a cotton sweater for her husband, but all the sweaters are wool.

She's looking for an inexpensive bracelet for her sister, but all the bracelets are expensive. She's looking for a leather purse for her mother, but all the purses are vinyl. And she's looking for a polka dot tie for her father, but all the ties are striped.

Poor Mrs. Miller is very frustrated. She's looking for special gifts for all the special people in her family, but she's having a lot of trouble.

✔ READING *CHECK-UP*

Q & A

Mrs. Miller is in the department store. Using this model, create dialogs based on the story.

  A. Excuse me. I'm looking for *a brown umbrella* for my *son.*
  B. I'm sorry. All our *umbrellas* are *black.*

LISTENING

WHAT'S THE WORD?

Listen and choose the correct answer.

1. a. blouse   b. dress
2. a. shoes   b. boots
3. a. necklace   b. bracelet
4. a. coat   b. raincoat
5. a. socks   b. stockings
6. a. shirt   b. skirt

WHICH WORD DO YOU HEAR?

Listen and choose the correct answer.

1. a. jacket   b. jackets
2. a. belt   b. belts
3. a. sweater   b. sweaters
4. a. suit   b. suits
5. a. shoe   b. shoes
6. a. tie   b. ties

PRONUNCIATION *Emphasized Words*

Listen. Then say it.

But this is a PURPLE jacket!

Green gloves are very POPULAR this year.

I think this is MY jacket.

THAT umbrella is BROWN, and
    MY umbrella is BLACK.

Say it. Then listen.

But these are YELLOW shoes!

Striped socks are very POPULAR this year.

I think these are MY glasses.

THOSE boots are DIRTY, and
    MY boots are CLEAN.

What are you wearing today? Tell
about the clothing and the colors.
Write about it in your journal.

GRAMMAR FOCUS

SINGULAR/PLURAL

[s]	I'm looking for **a** coat. Coat**s** are over there.
[z]	I'm looking for **an** umbrella. Umbrella**s** are over there.
[IZ]	I'm looking for **a** dress. Dress**es** are over there.

Choose the correct word.

1. A. May I help you?
   B. Yes. I'm looking for a (shirt   shirts).

2. A. Pants (is   are) over there.
   B. Thank you.

3. A. Can I help you?
   B. Yes. I'm looking for a (necklace   jeans).

4. A. May I help you?
   B. Yes. I'm looking for an (hat   umbrella).

5. A. (Blouse   Blouses) are over there.
   B. Thanks.

6. A. Can I help you?
   B. I'm looking for a pair of (gloves   earring).

7. A. Here's a nice (socks   dress).
   B. But this (socks   dress) (is   are) orange!

THIS/THAT/THESE/THOSE

Is **this** your umbrella?   **That** umbrella is brown.
Are **these** your boots?   **Those** boots are dirty.

ADJECTIVES

This is a **purple** jacket.   These are **green** gloves.

8. Is (this   these) your jacket?

9. (That   Those) are my gloves.

10. This isn't my coat. (That's   This) my coat.

11. (These   This) briefcase is black.

12. (Those are   That's) yellow ties.

13. (That's   Those are) my purse.

14. (This   These) are my (mitten   mittens).

Clothing, Colors, and Cultures

Blue and pink aren't children's clothing colors all around the world

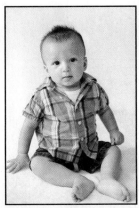
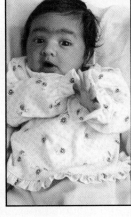

The meanings of colors are sometimes very different in different cultures. For example, in some cultures, blue is a common clothing color for little boys, and pink is a common clothing color for little girls. In other cultures, other colors are common for boys and girls.

There are also different colors for special days in different cultures. For example, white is the traditional color of a wedding dress in some cultures, but other colors are traditional in other cultures.

For some people, white is a happy color. For others, it's a sad color. For some people, red is a beautiful and lucky color. For others, it's a very sad color.

What are the meanings of different colors in YOUR culture?

LISTENING

Attention, J-Mart Shoppers!

_c_	❶ jackets	**a.**	Aisle 1
____	❷ gloves	**b.**	Aisle 7
____	❸ blouses	**c.**	Aisle 9
____	❹ bracelets	**d.**	Aisle 11
____	❺ ties	**e.**	Aisle 5

That's a very nice _____ .

 ■ bathrobe

 ■ tee shirt

 ■ scarf

 ■ wallet

 ■ ring

Those are very nice _____ .

 ■ sandals

 ■ slippers

 ■ sneakers

 ■ shorts

 ■ sweat pants

People's Homes

Homes are different all around the world.

This family is living in a farmhouse.

This family is living in a hut.

This family is living in a houseboat.

These people are living in a mobile home (a trailer).

What different kinds of homes are there in your country?

FACT FILE

Urban, Suburban, and Rural

urban areas	=	cities
suburban areas	=	places near cities
rural areas	=	places in the countryside, far from cities

About 50% (percent) of the world's population is in urban and suburban areas.

About 50% (percent) of the world's population is in rural areas.

urban and suburban | *rural*

Global Exchange

RosieM: My apartment is in a wonderful neighborhood. There's a big, beautiful park across from my apartment building. Around the corner, there's a bank, a post office, and a laundromat. There are also many restaurants and stores in my neighborhood. It's a noisy place, but it's a very interesting place. There are a lot of people on the sidewalks all day and all night. How about your neighborhood? Tell me about it.

Send a message to a keypal. Tell about your neighborhood.

What Are They Saying?

Simple Present Tense

- **Languages and Nationalities**
- **Everyday Activities**

VOCABULARY PREVIEW

1. call
2. cook
3. drive
4. eat
5. listen to music
6. paint
7. play
8. read
9. sell
10. shop
11. sing
12. speak
13. visit
14. watch TV
15. work

Interviews Around the World

I / We / You / They live.

Where do I / we / you / they live?

What do I / we / you / they do?

A. **What's your name?**

B. **My name is Antonio.**

A. **Where do you live?**

B. **I live in Rome.**

A. **What language do you speak?**

B. **I speak Italian.**

A. **Tell me, what do you do every day?**

B. **I eat Italian food,
I sing Italian songs,
and I watch Italian TV shows!**

Interview these people.

What's your name?
Where do you live?
What language do you speak?
What do you do every day?

1. Spanish — MADRID — Carmen

2. Japanese — TOKYO — Kenji

3. French — PARIS — Nicole

4. German — BERLIN — Erik and Monika

5. Korean — SEOUL — Jae Hee

6. Russian — MOSCOW — Boris and Natasha

People Around the World

He	
She	lives.
It	

Where does { he / she / it } live?

What does { he / she / it } do?

MEXICO CITY

A. What's his name?

B. His name is Miguel.

A. Where does he live?

B. He lives in Mexico City.

A. What language does he speak?

B. He speaks Spanish.

A. What does he do every day?

B. He eats Mexican food,
he reads Mexican newspapers,
and he listens to Mexican music.

Ask and answer questions about these people.

What's his/her name?
Where does he/she live?
What language does he/she speak?
What does he/she do every day?

1. Kate — TORONTO — English, Canadian

2. Carlos — SAN JUAN — Spanish, Puerto Rican

3. Anna — ATHENS — Greek

4. Ming — HONG KONG — Chinese

5. Sonia — RIO de JANEIRO — Portuguese, Brazilian

6. Omar — CAIRO — Arabic, Egyptian

TALK ABOUT IT! *Where Do They Live, and What Do They Do?*

I We You They } live.		do { I we you they	
He She It } lives.	Where	does { he she it	live?

do { I we you they	
What	does { he she it } do?

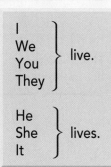

My name is Linda.
I live in London.
I work in a library.

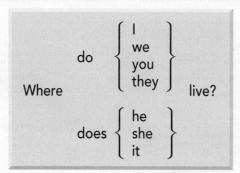

My name is Brian.
I live in Boston.
I work in a bank.

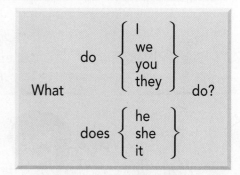

We're Walter and Wendy.
We live in Washington, D.C.
We work in an office.

My name is Bob.
I live in Buffalo.
I drive a bus.

We're Howard and Henry.
We live in Honolulu.
We paint houses.

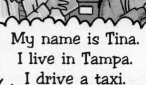

My name is Tina.
I live in Tampa.
I drive a taxi.

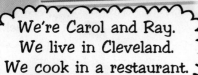

We're Carol and Ray.
We live in Cleveland.
We cook in a restaurant.

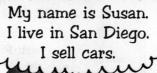

My name is Susan.
I live in San Diego.
I sell cars.

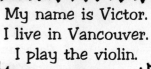

My name is Victor.
I live in Vancouver.
I play the violin.

Use these models to talk with other students about the people above.

A. Where does *Linda* live?
B. *She* lives in *London*.
A. What does *she* do?
B. *She works in a library*.

A. Where do *Walter* and *Wendy* live?
B. They live in *Washington, D.C.*
A. What do they do?
B. They *work in an office*.

How About You?

Where do you live?
What do you do?

MR. AND MRS. DiCARLO

Mr. and Mrs. DiCarlo live in an old Italian neighborhood in New York City. They speak a little English, but usually they speak Italian.

They read the Italian newspaper. They listen to Italian radio programs. They shop at the Italian grocery store around the corner from their apartment building. And every day they visit their friends and neighbors and talk about life back in "the old country."

Mr. and Mrs. DiCarlo are upset about their son, Joe. He lives in a small suburb outside the city. He speaks a little Italian, but usually he speaks English. He reads American newspapers. He listens to American radio programs. He shops at big suburban supermarkets and shopping malls. And when he visits his friends and neighbors, he always speaks English.

In fact, Joe speaks Italian only when he calls his parents on the telephone, or when he visits them every weekend.

Mr. and Mrs. DiCarlo are sad because their son speaks so little Italian. They're afraid he's forgetting his language, his culture, and his country.

✔ READING CHECK-UP

WHAT'S THE ANSWER?

1. Where do Mr. and Mrs. DiCarlo live?
2. Where does Joe live?
3. What language do Mr. and Mrs. DiCarlo usually speak?
4. What language does Joe usually speak?
5. What do Mr. and Mrs. DiCarlo read?
6. What does Joe read?

7. What do Mr. and Mrs. DiCarlo listen to?
8. What does Joe listen to?
9. Where do Mr. and Mrs. DiCarlo shop?
10. Where does Joe shop?

WHICH WORD IS CORRECT?

1. Mrs. DiCarlo (read   reads) the Italian newspaper.
2. Mr. DiCarlo (shop   shops) at the Italian grocery store.
3. They (live   lives) in New York City.
4. Joe (live   lives) outside the city.
5. He (speak   speaks) English.
6. Mr. and Mrs. DiCarlo (listen   listens) to the radio.
7. They (visit   visits) their friends every day.
8. Their friends (talk   talks) about life back in "the old country."
9. Joe (call   calls) his parents on the telephone.
10. Joe's friends (speak   speaks) English.

LISTENING

Listen and choose the correct answer.

1. a. live   b. lives
2. a. work   b. works
3. a. speak   b. speaks
4. a. drive   b. drives
5. a. read   b. reads

6. a. visit   b. visits
7. a. cook   b. cooks
8. a. paint   b. paints
9. a. call   b. calls
10. a. shop   b. shops

How to Say It!

Hesitating

A. What do you do every day?
B. Hmm. Well . . .
   I *work*, I *read the newspaper*, and I *visit my friends*.

Practice conversations with other students. Hesitate while you're thinking of your answer.

IN YOUR OWN WORDS

MRS. KOWALSKI

Mrs. Kowalski lives in an old Polish neighborhood in Chicago. She's upset about her son, Michael, and his wife, Kathy. Using the story on page 83 as a model, tell a story about Mrs. Kowalski.

INTERVIEW

Where do you live?
What language do you speak?
What do you do every day?

Interview another student.

I live in an apartment in the city.
I speak Spanish and a little English.
I go to school and visit my friends.

Then tell the class about that person.

She lives in an apartment in the city.
She speaks Spanish and a little English.
She goes to school and visits her friends.

85

PRONUNCIATION Blending with *does*

Listen. Then say it.

Where does he work?

Where does she live?

What does he do?

What does she read?

Say it. Then listen.

Where does he shop?

Where does she eat?

What does he cook?

What does she talk about?

Where do you live? What language do you speak? What do you do every day? Write a paragraph about it in your journal.

GRAMMAR FOCUS

SIMPLE PRESENT TENSE

Where	do	I we you they	live?
	does	he she it	

I We You They	live	in Rome.
He She It	lives	

Match the questions and answers.

____ 1. Where do you and your wife live?

____ 2. Where does your brother live?

____ 3. Where do your parents live?

____ 4. Where does your sister live?

____ 5. Where do you live?

a. They live in Mexico City.

b. I live in Chicago.

c. She lives in Los Angeles.

d. We live in Dallas.

e. He lives in London.

Choose the correct word.

6. He (drive   drives) a truck.

7. We (speak   speaks) Portuguese.

8. I (sell   sells) cars.

9. They (read   reads) every day.

10. Where (do   does) they live?

11. Where (do   does) she work?

12. You (speak   speaks) Arabic.

13. She (listen   listens) to the radio.

14. Where (do   does) you work?

15. What language (do   does) you and your wife speak?

Simple Present Tense:
Yes/No Questions
Negatives
Short Answers

- **Habitual Actions**
- **People's Interests and Activities**

VOCABULARY PREVIEW

SUN	MON	TUE	WED	THU	FRI	SAT
①	②	③	④	⑤	⑥	⑦
1	2	3	4	5	6	7
8	9	10	11	12	13	14
15	16	17	18	19	20	21
22	23	24	25	26	27	28
29	30	31				

1. Sunday
2. Monday
3. Tuesday
4. Wednesday
5. Thursday
6. Friday
7. Saturday

8. baby-sit
9. clean
10. do yoga
11. go dancing
12. jog

13. play volleyball
14. ride
15. see a movie
16. see a play

87

Stanley's International Restaurant

He cooks.	Does he cook?	What kind of food
He doesn't cook.	Yes, he does.	When } does he cook?
(does not)	No, he doesn't.	

MONDAY	TUESDAY	WEDNESDAY	THURSDAY	FRIDAY	SATURDAY	SUNDAY
Italian	Greek	Chinese	Puerto Rican	Japanese	Mexican	American

Stanley's International Restaurant is a very special place. Every day Stanley cooks a different kind of food. On Monday he cooks Italian food. On Tuesday he cooks Greek food. On Wednesday he cooks Chinese food. On Thursday he cooks Puerto Rican food. On Friday he cooks Japanese food. On Saturday he cooks Mexican food. And on Sunday he cooks American food.

A. What kind of food does Stanley cook on **Monday**?

B. On **Monday** he cooks **Italian** food.

Ask and answer questions about the other days of the week.

A. Does Stanley cook **Greek** food on **Tuesday**?

B. Yes, he does.

Ask six questions with "yes" answers.

A. Does Stanley cook **Japanese** food on **Sunday**?

B. No, he doesn't.

A. When does he cook **Japanese** food?

B. He cooks **Japanese** food on **Friday**.

Ask six questions with "no" answers.

You go.
You don't go.
(do not)

Do you go?
Yes, I do. / Yes, we do.
No, I don't. / No, we don't.

When do you go?

A. Do you go to Stanley's Restaurant on **Wednesday**?

B. Yes, I do.

A. Why?

B. Because I like **Chinese** food.

Ask these people.

1. *Monday?*   **2.** *Thursday?*   **3.** *Saturday?*   **4.** *Sunday?*

A. Do you go to Stanley's Restaurant on **Sunday**?

B. No, I don't.

A. Why not?

B. Because I don't like **American** food.

Ask these people.

5. *Tuesday?*   **6.** *Wednesday?*   **7.** *Friday?*   **8.** *Monday?*

A. What kind of food do you like?

B. I like **Russian** food.

A. When do you go to Stanley's Restaurant?

B. I don't go there.

A. Why not?

B. Because Stanley doesn't cook **Russian** food.

Ask these people.

9. *French*   **10.** *Ethiopian*   **11.** *Thai*   **12.** *Vietnamese*

Busy People!

| MONDAY | TUESDAY | WEDNESDAY | THURSDAY | FRIDAY | SATURDAY | SUNDAY |

Jeff is a very athletic person. He does a different kind of exercise or sport every day. On Monday he jogs. On Tuesday he plays tennis. On Wednesday he does yoga. On Thursday he swims. On Friday he goes to a health club. On Saturday he plays basketball. And on Sunday he rides his bike.

| MONDAY | TUESDAY | WEDNESDAY | THURSDAY | FRIDAY | SATURDAY | SUNDAY |

Julie is a very busy student. She does a different activity every day. On Monday she sings in the choir. On Tuesday she plays in the orchestra. On Wednesday she writes for the school newspaper. On Thursday she plays volleyball. On Friday she baby-sits for her neighbors. On Saturday she works at the mall. And on Sunday she visits her grandparents.

| MONDAY | TUESDAY | WEDNESDAY | THURSDAY | FRIDAY | SATURDAY | SUNDAY |

Mr. and Mrs. Baker are very active people. They do something different every day of the week. On Monday they go to a museum. On Tuesday they see a play. On Wednesday they go to a concert. On Thursday they take a karate lesson. On Friday they go dancing. On Saturday they see a movie. And on Sunday they play cards with their friends.

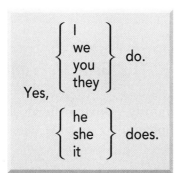

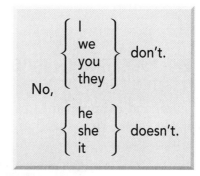

A. Does Jeff play tennis on Tuesday?

B. Yes, he does.

A. Does Julie work at the mall on Saturday?

B. Yes, she does.

A. Do Mr. and Mrs. Baker go dancing on Friday?

B. Yes, they do.

Ask other questions with "yes" answers.

A. Does Jeff do yoga on Sunday?

B. No, he doesn't.

A. Does Julie sing in the choir on Thursday?

B. No, she doesn't.

A. Do Mr. and Mrs. Baker see a movie on Monday?

B. No, they don't.

Ask other questions with "no" answers.

Now interview Jeff, Julie, and Mr. and Mrs. Baker. Practice conversations with other students.

EVERY WEEKEND IS IMPORTANT TO THE GARCIA FAMILY

Every weekend is important to the Garcia family. During the week they don't have very much time together, but they spend a LOT of time together on the weekend.

Mr. Garcia works at the post office during the week, but he doesn't work there on the weekend. Mrs. Garcia works at the bank during the week, but she doesn't work there on the weekend. Jennifer and Jonathan Garcia go to school during the week, but they don't go to school on the weekend. And the Garcias' dog, Max, stays home alone during the week, but he doesn't stay home alone on the weekend.

On Saturday and Sunday the Garcias spend time together. On Saturday morning they clean the house together. On Saturday afternoon they work in the garden together. And on Saturday evening they watch videos together. On Sunday morning they go to church together. On Sunday afternoon they have a big dinner together. And on Sunday evening they play their musical instruments together.

As you can see, every weekend is special to the Garcias. It's their only time together as a family.

✓ READING CHECK-UP

Q & A

Using these models, make questions and answers based on the story on page 92.

A. What *does Mr. Garcia* do during the week?
B. *He works at the post office.*

A. What do the Garcias do on *Saturday morning*?
B. They *clean the house* together.

DO OR DOES?

1. _____ Mr. Garcia work on the weekend?
2. _____ Jennifer and Jonathan go to school during the week?
3. When _____ they watch videos?
4. Where _____ Mrs. Garcia work?
5. _____ you speak Spanish?
6. What _____ Mr. Garcia do during the week?

WHAT'S THE ANSWER?

1. Does Mr. Garcia work at the post office?
2. Do Jennifer and Jonathan go to school during the week?
3. Does Mrs. Garcia work at the post office?
4. Do Mr. and Mrs. Garcia have much time together during the week?
5. Does Jennifer watch videos on Saturday evening?
6. Do Jennifer and her brother clean the house on Saturday morning?
7. Does Mr. Garcia work in the garden on Saturday evening?

DON'T OR DOESN'T?

1. Mr. and Mrs. Garcia _____ work on the weekend.
2. Jennifer _____ work at the bank.
3. We _____ watch videos during the week.
4. My son _____ play a musical instrument.
5. My sister and I _____ eat at Stanley's Restaurant.
6. Our dog _____ like our neighbor's dog.

LISTENING

WHAT'S THE WORD?

Listen and choose the word you hear.

1. a. do   b. does
2. a. do   b. does
3. a. Sunday   b. Monday
4. a. don't   b. doesn't
5. a. don't   b. doesn't
6. a. does   b. goes
7. a. Tuesday   b. Thursday
8. a. go   b. don't

WHAT'S THE ANSWER?

Listen and choose the correct response.

1. a. Yes, I do.   b. Yes, he does.
2. a. Yes, they do.   b. Yes, she does.
3. a. No, she doesn't. b. No, we don't.
4. a. No, he doesn't.   b. No, we don't.
5. a. No, I don't.   b. No, he doesn't.
6. a. No, I don't.   b. No, they don't.
7. a. Yes, we do.   b. Yes, they do.
8. a. Yes, they do.   b. Yes, he does.

How About You?

Tell about yourself:
What do you do during the week?
What do you do on the weekend?

Now tell about another person—a friend, someone in your family, or another student:
What does he/she do during the week?
What does he/she do on the weekend?

READING

A VERY OUTGOING PERSON

Alice is a very outgoing person. She spends a lot of time with her friends. She goes to parties, she goes to movies, and she goes to concerts. She's very popular.

She also likes sports very much. She plays basketball, she plays baseball, and she plays volleyball. She's very athletic.

Alice doesn't stay home alone very often. She doesn't read many books, she doesn't watch TV, and she doesn't listen to music. She's very active.

As you can see, Alice is a very outgoing person.

IN YOUR OWN WORDS

For Writing and Discussion

A VERY SHY PERSON

Using the story about Alice as a model, tell a story about Sheldon. Begin your story:

Sheldon is a very shy person. He doesn't spend a lot of time with his friends. He doesn't go . . .

How About You?

Tell about yourself:
   What kind of person are you?
   Are you outgoing? shy? active? athletic?
   Tell how you spend your time.

How to Say It!

Starting a Conversation

A. Tell me, what kind of *movies* do you like?
B. I like *comedies*.
A. Who's your favorite *movie star*?
B. *Tim Kelly*.

Practice the interviews on this page, using "Tell me" to start the conversations.

INTERVIEW

First, answer these questions about yourself. Next, interview another student.
Then, tell the class about yourself and the other student.

1. What kind of movies do you like?

   Who's your favorite movie star?

   comedies   dramas   westerns   adventure movies   science fiction movies   cartoons

2. What kind of books do you like?

   Who's your favorite author?

   novels   poetry   short stories   non-fiction   biographies

3. What kind of TV programs do you like?

   Who's your favorite TV star?

   comedies   dramas   cartoons   game shows   news programs

4. What kind of music do you like?

   Who's your favorite performer?

   classical music   popular music   jazz   rock music   country music

5. What kind of sports do you like?

   Who's your favorite athlete? What's your favorite team?

   football   baseball   soccer   golf   hockey   tennis

PRONUNCIATION Reduced *of*

Listen. Then say it.

What kind of movies do you like?

What kind of books do you like?

She spends a lot of time with her friends.

Say it. Then listen.

What kind of music do you like?

What kind of TV programs do you like?

I read a lot of books.

SIDE by SIDE JOURNAL

What do you do during the week?
What do you do on the weekend?
Write about it in your journal.

GRAMMAR FOCUS

SIMPLE PRESENT TENSE:
YES/NO QUESTIONS

Do	I we you they	work?
Does	he she it	

SHORT ANSWERS

Yes,	I we you they	do.
	he she it	does.

No,	I we you they	don't.
	he she it	doesn't.

Complete the sentences.

1. A. _____ you and your wife like Italian food?
   B. Yes, we _____.

2. A. _____ your brother work at the mall?
   B. Yes, he _____.

3. A. _____ your friends play cards?
   B. No, they _____.

4. A. _____ you play a musical instrument?
   B. Yes, I _____.

5. A. _____ your sister take karate lessons?
   B. No, she _____.

6. A. _____ I ask a lot of questions?
   B. Yes, you _____.

7. A. _____ you and your husband play golf?
   B. No, _____ _____.

8. A. _____ your uncle speak French?
   B. No, _____ _____.

9. A. Do your neighbors make a lot of noise?
   B. Yes, _____ _____.

10. A. _____ your daughter speak Chinese?
    B. Yes, _____ _____.

SIMPLE PRESENT TENSE: NEGATIVES

I We You They	don't	work.
He She It	doesn't	

Complete the sentences with *don't* or *doesn't*.

11. I _____ work on Sunday.

12. My husband _____ play tennis.

13. My parents _____ go dancing.

14. My sister and I _____ sing in the choir.

15. My wife _____ watch TV.

16. You _____ like hockey.

96

Volume 1   Number 4

Language

Millions speak Chinese. Only hundreds speak Bahinemo.

There are over 20,000 languages in the world. Some of these languages are very common. For example, millions of people speak Chinese, Spanish, English, Arabic, Portuguese, and Japanese. On the other hand, some languages are very rare. For example, only 500 people in Papua, New Guinea speak the language Bahinemo.

Languages grow and change. They borrow words from other languages. For example, in the English language, the word *rodeo* is from Spanish, *cafe* comes from French, *ketchup* is from Chinese, *sofa* is from Arabic, and *potato* comes from Haitian Kreyol. New words also come from technology. For example, *cyberspace*, *website*, and *e-mail* are recent words that relate to the Internet.

FACT FILE

Common Languages

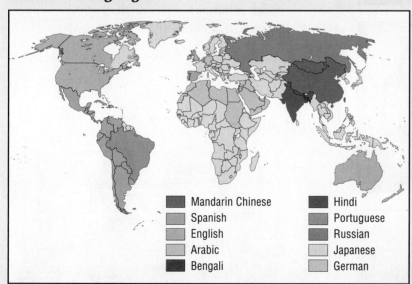

Mandarin Chinese
Spanish
English
Arabic
Bengali

Hindi
Portuguese
Russian
Japanese
German

Language	Number of Speakers	Language	Number of Speakers
Mandarin Chinese	885 million	Hindi	182 million
Spanish	332 million	Portuguese	170 million
English	322 million	Russian	170 million
Arabic	268 million	Japanese	125 million
Bengali	189 million	German	98 million

BUILD YOUR VOCABULARY!

Everyday Activities

Every day I _____ .

 get up

 take a shower

 brush my teeth

 comb my hair

 get dressed

 go to school

 go to work

 eat

 take a bath

 go to bed

AROUND THE WORLD

Exercising

People around the world exercise in different ways.

Some people exercise in health clubs.

Some people exercise at the beach.

Some people go hiking.

And some people exercise together outdoors.

How do people exercise in your country?

Send a message to a keypal. Tell about your activities and interests.

LISTENING

Hello! This Is the International Cafe!

_c_	**1**	Monday	**a.**	jazz
___	**2**	Tuesday	**b.**	rock music
___	**3**	Wednesday	**c.**	classical music
___	**4**	Thursday	**d.**	popular music
___	**5**	Friday	**e.**	poetry
___	**6**	Saturday	**f.**	country music
___	**7**	Sunday	**g.**	short stories

What Are They Saying?

Object Pronouns
Simple Present Tense: -s vs. non-s Endings
Have/Has
Adverbs of Frequency

- Describing Frequency of Actions
- Describing People

VOCABULARY PREVIEW

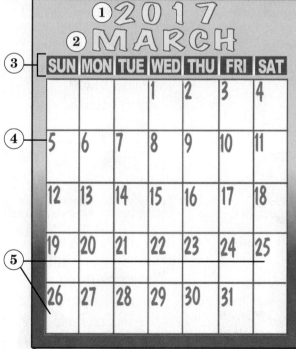

1. year
2. month
3. week
4. day
5. weekend

6. morning
7. afternoon
8. evening
9. night

How Often?

I	me
he	him
she	her
it	it
we	us
you	you
they	them

A. How often does your boyfriend call you?

B. He calls me every night.

1. How often do you use your computer?
every day

2. How often do you write to your son?
every week

3. How often do you clean your windows?
every month

4. How often do you visit your aunt in Minnesota?
every year

5. How often do you wash your car?
every weekend

6. How often do your grandchildren call you?
every Sunday

7. How often does your boss say "hello" to you?
every morning

8. How often do you feed the animals?
every afternoon

9. How often do you think about me?
all the time

She Usually Studies in the Library

A. Does Carmen usually study in her room?

B. No. She rarely studies in her room. She usually studies in the library.

1. Does Linda usually eat lunch in her office?
rarely
in the cafeteria

2. Does Alan always watch the news after dinner?
never
game shows

3. Does Diane sometimes read *The National Star*?
never
Time magazine

4. Does Henry usually wash his car on Sunday?
rarely
on Saturday

5. Does your girlfriend usually jog in the evening?
sometimes
in the afternoon

6. Does your neighbor's dog always bark during the day?
never
at night

We Have Noisy Neighbors

I We You They } have	brown eyes.
He She It } has	

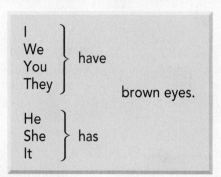

A. Do you have quiet neighbors?

B. No. We have noisy neighbors.

1. Do you have a sister?
   a brother

2. Does this store have an elevator?
   an escalator

3. Does your daughter have straight hair?
   curly hair

4. Does your son have brown hair?
   blond hair

5. Do you and your husband have a dog?
   a cat

6. Does your baby boy have blue eyes?
   brown eyes

7. Do Mr. and Mrs. Hill have a satellite dish?
   an old TV antenna

8. Does your grandmother have a car?
   a motorcycle

9.

My brother and I look very different. I have brown eyes and he has blue eyes. We both have brown hair, but I have short, curly hair and he has long, straight hair. I'm tall and thin. He's short and heavy.

As you can see, I don't look like my brother. We look very different.

Who in your family do you look like? Who DON'T you look like? Tell about it.

My sister and I are very different. I'm a teacher. She's a journalist. I live in Miami. She lives in London. I have a large house in the suburbs. She has a small apartment in the city.

I'm married. She's single. I play golf. She plays tennis. I play the piano. She doesn't play a musical instrument. On the weekend I usually watch videos and rarely go out. She never watches videos and always goes to parties.

As you can see, we're very different. But we're sisters . . . and we're friends.

Compare yourself with a member of your family, another student in your class, or a famous person. Tell how you and this person are different.

How to Say It!

Reacting to Information

A. Tell me about *your sister.*

B. *She's a journalist. She lives in London.*

A. Oh, really? That's interesting.

Practice conversations with other students. Talk about people you know.

CLOSE FRIENDS

My husband and I are very lucky. We have many close friends in this city, and they're all interesting people.

Our friend Greta is an actress. We see her when she isn't making a movie in Hollywood. When we get together with her, she always tells us about her life in Hollywood as a movie star. Greta is a very close friend. We like her very much.

Our friend Dan is a scientist. We see him when he isn't busy in his laboratory. When we get together with him, he always tells us about his new experiments. Dan is a very close friend. We like him very much.

Our friends Bob and Carol are famous television news reporters. We see them when they aren't traveling around the world. When we get together with them, they always tell us about their conversations with presidents and prime ministers. Bob and Carol are very close friends. We like them very much.

Unfortunately, we don't see Greta, Dan, Bob, or Carol very often. In fact, we rarely see them because they're usually so busy. But we think about them all the time.

✔ READING CHECK-UP

WHAT'S THE WORD?

Greta is a famous actress. _____ ¹ lives in Hollywood. _____ ² movies are very popular. When _____ ³ walks down the street, people always say "hello" to _____ ⁴ and tell _____ ⁵ how much they like _____ ⁶ movies.

Dan is always busy. _____ ⁷ works in _____ ⁸ laboratory every day. Dan's friends rarely see _____ ⁹. When they see _____ ¹⁰, _____ ¹¹ usually talks about _____ ¹² experiments. Everybody likes _____ ¹³ very much. _____ ¹⁴ is a very nice person.

Bob and Carol are television news reporters. _____ ¹⁵ friends don't see _____ ¹⁶ very often because _____ ¹⁷ travel around the world all the time. Presidents and prime ministers often call _____ ¹⁸ on the telephone. _____ ¹⁹ like _____ ²⁰ work very much.

LISTENING

Listen to the conversations. Who and what are they talking about?

1. a. grandfather
   b. grandmother

2. a. window
   b. windows

3. a. brother
   b. sister

4. a. sink
   b. cars

5. a. neighbor
   b. neighbors

6. a. computer
   b. news reporter

7. a. game show
   b. car

8. a. Ms. Brown
   b. Mr. Wong

9. a. Ken
   b. Jim and Karen

IN YOUR OWN WORDS

FOR WRITING AND DISCUSSION

MY CLOSE FRIENDS

Tell about your close friends.

What are their names?
Where do they live?
What do they do?
When do you get together with them?
What do you talk about?

PRONUNCIATION   Deleted *h*

Listen. Then say it.

I visit her every year.

I write to him every week.

We see her very often.

She calls him every month.

Say it. Then listen.

I visit him every year.

I write to her every week.

We see him very often.

He calls her every month.

 SIDE by SIDE JOURNAL

Write in your journal about your daily activities.

I always _____. I usually _____.

I sometimes _____. I rarely _____. I never _____.

GRAMMAR FOCUS

OBJECT PRONOUNS

He calls	me him her it us you them	every night.

Complete the sentences.

1. A. How often do you and your wife read the newspaper?
   B. We read _____ every morning.
2. A. How often do you write to your grandmother?
   B. I write to _____ every week.
3. A. How often do you call your brother in Miami?
   B. I call _____ every Sunday.
4. A. How often do the Baxters play cards with their friends?
   B. They play cards with _____ every Saturday night.
5. A. How often does your uncle call you and your sister?
   B. He calls _____ every weekend.

HAVE/HAS

I We You They	have	brown eyes.
He She It	has	

Complete the sentences with *have* or *has*.

6. We _____ noisy neighbors.
7. My son _____ brown eyes.
8. I _____ curly black hair.
9. My sister _____ a new car.
10. You _____ a very nice apartment.
11. My parents _____ a new cat.
12. The new mall _____ more than fifty stores.

SIMPLE PRESENT TENSE: *s* VS. NON-*s* ENDINGS

He She It	eats. reads. washes.	[s] [z] [ɪz]

I We You They	eat. read. wash.

Complete the sentences with the correct form of the verb.

13. (like) I _____ jazz. My brother _____ rock music.
14. (jog) My wife _____ in the morning. I _____ in the afternoon.
15. (study) I _____ in my room. My sister _____ in the library.
16. (watch) Our son _____ game shows after dinner. My wife and I _____ the news.

Contrast:
Simple Present and Present Continuous Tenses
Adjectives

- **Feelings and Emotions**
- **Describing Usual and Unusual Activities**

VOCABULARY PREVIEW

1. happy
2. sad
3. hungry
4. thirsty
5. hot
6. cold
7. tired
8. sick
9. angry
10. nervous
11. scared
12. embarrassed

I Always Cry When I'm Sad

cry
crying

A. Why are you crying?

B. I'm crying because I'm sad.
I ALWAYS cry when I'm sad.

smile
smiling

A. Why is she smiling?

B. She's smiling because she's happy.
She ALWAYS smiles when she's happy.

shout
shouting

1. A. Why are you shouting?

 B. _____ angry.

 I ALWAYS _____.

bite
biting

2. A. Why is he biting his nails?

 B. _____ nervous.

 He ALWAYS _____.

drink
drinking

3. A. Why is the bird drinking?

 B. _____ thirsty.

 It ALWAYS _____.

shiver
shivering

4. A. Why are they shivering?

 B. _____ cold.

 They ALWAYS _____.

go
going

5. A. Why are they going to
Stanley's Restaurant?

 B. _____ hungry.

 They ALWAYS _____.

go
going

6. A. Why is she going to
the doctor?

 B. _____ sick.

 She ALWAYS _____.

perspire
perspiring

7. **A.** Why are you perspiring?

   B. _____ hot.

     I ALWAYS _____.

blush
blushing

8. **A.** Why is he blushing?

   B. _____ embarrassed.

     He ALWAYS _____.

yawn
yawning

9. **A.** Why is she yawning?

   B. _____ tired.

     She ALWAYS _____.

cover
covering

10. **A.** Why is he covering his eyes?

    B. _____ scared.

      He ALWAYS _____.

ON YOUR OWN *What Do You Do When You're Nervous?*

What do you do when you're nervous?

When I'm nervous, I perspire.

When I'm nervous, I bite my nails.

When I'm nervous, I walk back and forth.

Answer these questions.

What do you do when you're . . .

1. nervous?	5. sick?	9. thirsty?
2. sad?	6. cold?	10. angry?
3. happy?	7. hot?	11. embarrassed?
4. tired?	8. hungry?	12. scared?

Now ask another student in your class.

I'm Washing the Dishes in the Bathtub

A. What are you doing?!

B. I'm washing the dishes in the bathtub.

A. That's strange! Do you USUALLY wash the dishes in the bathtub?

B. No. I NEVER wash the dishes in the bathtub, but I'm washing the dishes in the bathtub TODAY.

A. Why are you doing THAT?!

B. Because my sink is broken.

A. I'm sorry to hear that.

A. What are you doing?!

B. I'm _____.

A. That's strange! Do you USUALLY _____?

B. No. I NEVER _____, but I'm _____ TODAY.

A. Why are you doing THAT?!

B. Because my _____ is broken.

A. I'm sorry to hear that.

1. *sleep*
sleeping } *on the floor*
bed

2. *study*
studying } *with a*
flashlight
lamp

3. *walk*
walking } *to work*
car

4. *use*
using } *a typewriter*
computer

5. *sweep*
sweeping } *the carpet*
vacuum

6.

How to Say It!

Reacting to Bad News

A. *My sink is broken.*

B. { I'm sorry to hear that.
That's too bad!
What a shame!

Practice conversations with other students. Share some bad news and react to it.

A BAD DAY AT THE OFFICE

Mr. Blaine is the president of the Acme Internet Company. The company has a staff of energetic employees. Unfortunately, all of the employees are out today. Nobody is there. As a result, Mr. Blaine is doing everybody's job, and he's having a VERY bad day at the office!

He's answering the telephone because the receptionist who usually answers it is at the dentist's office. He's typing letters because the secretary who usually types them is at home in bed with the flu. He's sorting the mail because the office assistant who usually sorts it is on vacation. And he's even cleaning the office because the custodian who usually cleans it is on strike.

Poor Mr. Blaine! It's a very busy day at the Acme Internet Company, and nobody is there to help him. He's having a VERY bad day at the office!

 READING *CHECK-UP*

TRUE OR FALSE?

1. Mr. Blaine is the president of the Ajax Internet Company.
2. Mr. Blaine is out today.
3. The secretary is sick.
4. The office assistant is on strike.
5. The custodian isn't cleaning the office today.
6. The receptionist usually answers the phone at the dentist's office.

LISTENING

Listen and choose the correct answer.

1. a. I clean my house.
   b. I'm cleaning my house.
2. a. He sorts the mail.
   b. He's sorting the mail.
3. a. She answers the telephone.
   b. She's answering the telephone.
4. a. Yes. He yawns.
   b. Yes. He's yawning.
5. a. I'm covering my eyes.
   b. I cover my eyes.
6. a. I study in the library.
   b. I'm studying in the library.

EARLY MONDAY MORNING IN CENTERVILLE

   Early Monday morning is usually a very busy time in Centerville. Men and women usually rush to their jobs. Some people walk to work, some people drive, and others take the bus. Children usually go to school. Some children walk to school, some children take the school bus, and others ride their bicycles. The city is usually very busy. Trucks deliver food to supermarkets, mail carriers deliver mail to homes and businesses, and police officers direct traffic at every corner. Yes, early Monday morning is usually a very busy time in Centerville.

✓ READING *CHECK-UP*

Using the story above as a guide, complete the following:

THE SNOWSTORM

   Today isn't a typical early Monday morning in Centerville. In fact, it's a very unusual morning. It's snowing very hard there. All the people are at home. The streets are empty, and the city is quiet. The men and women who usually rush to their jobs aren't rushing to their jobs today. The people who usually walk to work aren't walking, the people who usually drive aren't _____¹, and the people who usually take the bus aren't _____² the bus. The children who usually go to school aren't _____³ to school today. The children who usually walk to school aren't _____⁴ today. The children who usually _____⁵ the school bus aren't _____⁶ it today. And the children who usually _____⁷ their bicycles aren't _____⁸ them this morning.

   The city is very quiet. The trucks that usually _____⁹ food aren't _____¹⁰ it today. The mail carriers who usually _____¹¹ mail aren't _____¹² it this morning. And the police officers who usually_____¹³ traffic aren't _____¹⁴ it today. Yes, it's a very unusual Monday morning in Centerville.

PRONUNCIATION   Reduced *to*

Listen. Then say it.

I'm sorry to hear that.

We go to school.

He listens to the radio.

Mail carriers deliver mail to homes.

Say it. Then listen.

I'm happy to hear that.

They're going to the doctor.

She listens to music.

Trucks deliver food to supermarkets.

Describe a typical day in your city or town. What do people usually do? Write about it in your journal.

GRAMMAR FOCUS

SIMPLE PRESENT TENSE

I always **cry** when I'm sad.

I never **wash** the dishes in the bathtub.

PRESENT CONTINUOUS TENSE

I'm **crying** because I'm sad.

I'm **washing** the dishes in the bathtub today.

Complete the sentences with the correct form of the verb.

bite	clean	shiver	smile	walk
biting	cleaning	shivering	smiling	walking
blush	cry	shout	use	yawn
blushing	crying	shouting	using	yawning

1. I often _____ when I'm sad.

2. Why are you _____? Are you angry?

3. Carol is _____. She's very tired.

4. He's _____ because he's happy.

5. I'm _____ my office today because the people who usually _____ it are on strike.

6. When I'm nervous, I _____ my nails.

7. I _____ when I'm embarrassed.

8. Why are you _____ a typewriter today?

9. I usually _____ when I'm very cold.

10. I don't usually _____ to work, but I'm _____ to work today.

BUILD YOUR VOCABULARY!
How Do You Get to Work?

Traffic: A Global Problem

There are more and more people and more and more cars

Traffic is a big problem in many cities around the world. Traffic is especially bad during *rush hour*—the time when people go to work or school and the time when they go home. Many people take buses, subways, or trains to work, but many other people drive their cars. As a result, the streets are very busy, and traffic is very bad.

Many cities are trying to solve their traffic problems. Some cities are building more roads. Other cities are expanding their bus and subway systems.

Many cities are trying to reduce the number of cars on their roads. Some highways have *carpool lanes*—special lanes for cars with two, three, or more people. In some cities, people drive their cars only on certain days of the week. For example, in Athens, people with license plate numbers ending in 0 through 4 drive on some days, and people with numbers ending in 5 through 9 drive on other days.

Every day around the world, more and more people drive to and from work in more and more cars. As a result, traffic is a global problem.

LISTENING

And Now, Here's Today's News!

TODAY'S NEWS

__b__ ❶ There's a subway problem in . . .   **a.** Toronto

____ ❷ Police officers are on strike in . . .   **b.** Boston

____ ❸ It's snowing very hard in . . .   **c.** Miami

____ ❹ There aren't any problems in . . .   **d.** Sacramento

____ ❺ Children aren't going to school in . . .   **e.** Chicago

I _____ .

 ■ walk

 ■ drive

 ■ take the bus

 ■ take the train

 ■ take the subway

 ■ take a taxi

 ■ ride a bicycle

 ■ ride a motor scooter

 ■ ride a motorcycle

AROUND THE WORLD

Getting Places

People around the world go to work or school in many different ways.

Some people take the subway.

Some people ride a bicycle.

Some people ride a motor scooter.

Some people even roller-blade!

How do people go to work or school in different countries you know?

FACT FILE

World's Largest Subway Systems

City	Number of Riders in a Year (in millions)	City	Number of Riders in a Year (in millions)
Moscow	3,160	Paris	1,120
Tokyo	2,740	Osaka	1,000
Mexico City	1,420	Hong Kong	779
Seoul	1,390	London	770
New York	1,130	Sao Paulo	701

Global Exchange

JeffZ: I live in a small apartment in the center of our city. I have a brother and two sisters. My brother's name is Kevin, and my sisters' names are Emily and Melissa. Our family has a dog and a bird. Our dog's name is Buster, and our bird's name is Lulu. I'm tall, and I have brown eyes. My hair is short and curly. It's usually black, but this week it's red. How about you? Where do you live? Do you have brothers or sisters? What are their names? Do you have a dog or a cat or another pet? What do you look like?

Send a message to a keypal. Tell about yourself.

What Are They Saying?

Can
Have to

- **Expressing Ability**
- **Occupations**
- **Looking for a Job**
- **Expressing Obligation**
- **Invitations**

VOCABULARY PREVIEW

1. actor
2. actress
3. baker
4. chef
5. construction worker
6. dancer
7. mechanic
8. salesperson
9. secretary
10. singer
11. superintendent
12. teacher
13. truck driver

Can You?

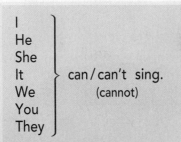

| I
He
She
It
We
You
They | can / can't sing.
(cannot) |

Can you sing?
Yes, I can.
No, I can't.

Can you speak Hungarian?

No, I can't. But I can speak Romanian.

1. Can Betty drive a bus?

2. Can Fred cook Italian food?

3. Can they ski?

4. Can you skate?

5. Can Roger use a cash register?

6. Can Judy and Donna play baseball?

7. Can Rita play the trumpet?

8. Can Marvin paint pictures?

Ask another student in your class: "Can you _____?"

Of Course They Can

A. Can Jack fix cars?

B. Of course he can.
He fixes cars every day. He's a mechanic.

1. Can Michael type?
secretary

2. Can Barbara teach?
teacher

3. Can Oscar bake pies and cakes?
baker

4. Can Jane drive a truck?
truck driver

5. Can Stanley cook?
chef

6. Can Claudia sing?
singer

7. Can Bruce and Helen dance?
dancers

8. Can Arthur act?
actor

9. Can Elizabeth and Katherine act?
actresses

THE ACE EMPLOYMENT SERVICE

Many people are sitting in the reception room at the Ace Employment Service. They're all looking for work, and they're hoping they can find jobs today.

Natalie is looking for a job as a secretary. She can type, she can file, and she can use business software on the computer. William is looking for a job as a building superintendent. He can paint walls, he can repair locks, and he can fix stoves and refrigerators.

Sandra is looking for a job as a construction worker. She can use tools, she can operate equipment, and she can build things. Nick is looking for a job as a salesperson. He can talk to customers, he can use a cash register, and he can take inventory. Stephanie and Tiffany are looking for jobs as actresses. They can sing, they can dance, and they can act.

Good luck, everybody! We hope you find the jobs you're looking for!

✔ READING CHECK-UP

Q & A

Natalie, William, Sandra, Nick, Stephanie, and Tiffany are having their interviews at the Ace Employment Service. Using this model, create dialogs based on the story.

A. What's your name?
B. *Natalie Kramer.*
A. Nice to meet you. Tell me, *Natalie*, what kind of job are you looking for?
B. I'm looking for a job as *a secretary*.
A. Tell me about your skills. What can you do?
B. I can *type*, I can *file*, and I can *use business software on the computer*.

LISTENING

CAN OR CAN'T?

Listen and choose the word you hear.

1. a. can   b. can't
2. a. can   b. can't
3. a. can   b. can't
4. a. can   b. can't
5. a. can   b. can't
6. a. can   b. can't

WHAT CAN THEY DO?

Listen and choose what each person can do.

1. a. file   b. type
2. a. cook   b. bake
3. a. repair locks b. repair stoves
4. a. drive a truck b. drive a bus
5. a. teach French b. teach English
6. a. take inventory b. paint

ON YOUR OWN *Your Skills*

I can paint.

I can't operate equipment.

I can use a computer.

I can't dance.

Things I Can Do	Things I Can't Do
....	....
....	....
....	....
....	....
....	....

Think about your skills. What can you do? What CAN'T you do? Make two lists. Then talk about your lists with other students.

They Can't Go to Herbert's Party

I We You They	have to	work.
He She It	has to	

Herbert is depressed. He's having a party today, but his friends can't go to his party. They're all busy.

A. Can you go to Herbert's party?

B. No, I can't. I have to work.

A. Can Michael go to Herbert's party?

B. No, he can't. He has to go to the doctor.

1. *you and Tom?*
fix our car

2. *Susan?*
go to the dentist

3. *your children?*
do their homework

4. *John?*
wash his clothes

5. *your parents?*
clean their apartment

6. Can YOU go to Herbert's party?

Apologizing

A. Can you *go to a movie* with me on *Saturday*?
B. I'm sorry. I can't. I have to *clean my apartment*.

Practice the interactions on this page, using "I'm sorry" to apologize.

INTERACTIONS

A. Can you _____ with me on _____?
B. I'm sorry. I can't. I have to _____.

Practice conversations with other students. Practice inviting, apologizing, and giving reasons.

go to a soccer game

have lunch

have dinner

go swimming

go shopping

go dancing

go skating

go skiing

go bowling

APPLYING FOR A DRIVER'S LICENSE

Henry is annoyed. He's applying for a driver's license, and he's upset about all the things he has to do.

First, he has to go to the Motor Vehicles Department and pick up an application form. He can't ask for the form on the telephone, and he can't ask for it by mail. He has to go downtown and pick up the form in person.

He has to fill out the form in duplicate. He can't use a pencil. He has to use a pen. He can't use blue ink. He has to use black ink. And he can't write in script. He has to print.

He also has to attach two photographs to the application. They can't be old photographs. They have to be new. They can't be large. They have to be small. And they can't be black and white. They have to be color.

Then he has to submit his application. He has to wait in a long line to pay his application fee. He has to wait in another long line to have an eye examination. And believe it or not, he has to wait in ANOTHER long line to take a written test!

Finally, he has to take a road test. He has to start the car. He has to make a right turn, a left turn, and a U-turn. And he even has to park his car on a crowded city street.

No wonder Henry is annoyed! He's applying for his driver's license, and he can't believe all the things he has to do.

✓ READING *CHECK-UP*

WHAT'S THE ANSWER?

1. Can Henry apply for a driver's license on the telephone?
2. Where does he have to go to apply for a license?
3. How does he have to fill out the form?
4. How many photographs does he have to attach to the application?
5. What kind of photographs do they have to be?
6. What does Henry have to do during the road test?

FIX THIS SIGN!

This sign at the Motor Vehicles Department is wrong. The things people have to do are in the wrong order. On a separate sheet of paper, fix the sign based on the story.

> **How to Apply for a Driver's License**
>
> Have an eye examination.
> Pay the application fee.
> Take a road test.
> Pick up an application form.
> Take a written test.
> Fill out the form in duplicate.

IN YOUR OWN WORDS

FOR WRITING AND DISCUSSION

Explain how to apply for one of the following: a passport, a marriage license, a loan, or something else. In your explanation, use "You have to."*

* "You have to" = "A person has to"

Listen. Then say it.

I can type.

She can teach.

Yes, I can.

No, he can't.

Say it. Then listen.

We can dance.

He can sing.

Yes, they can.

No, she can't.

What do you have to do this week? Write about it in your journal.

GRAMMAR FOCUS

CAN

Can	I he she it we you they	sing?

	I He She It We You They	can can't	sing.

Yes,	I he she it we you they	can.

No,	I he she it we you they	can't.

HAVE TO

I We You They	have to	
He She It	has to	work.

Complete the sentences with *can* or *can't*.

1. I _____ bake. I'm a very good baker.

2. Gregory is a very bad singer. He _____ sing.

3. Maria can't ski, but she _____ skate.

4. We _____ dance. We aren't good dancers.

5. They can play baseball, but they _____ play tennis.

6. A. _____ you drive a truck?

   B. Yes, I _____ .

7. A. _____ your brother fix cars?

   B. No, he _____ .

8. A. _____ she repair stoves?

   B. No, she _____ , but she _____ repair locks.

Complete the sentences with *have to* or *has to*.

9. I can't go to your party. I _____ work.

10. Beth _____ go to the dentist today.

11. Mr. and Mrs. Shen _____ clean their apartment today.

12. Ruben _____ wash his clothes today.

13. We can't go swimming. We _____ fix our car.

14. Bobby, you can't go skating. You _____ do your homework.

Future: Going to
Time Expressions
Want to

- **Describing Future Plans and Intentions**
- **Expressing Wants**
- **Weather Forecasts**
- **Telling Time**
- **Making Predictions**

VOCABULARY PREVIEW

Time

2:00

It's two o'clock.

2:15

It's two fifteen.
It's a quarter after two.

2:30

It's two thirty.
It's half past two.

2:45

It's two forty-five.
It's a quarter to three.

Months of the Year

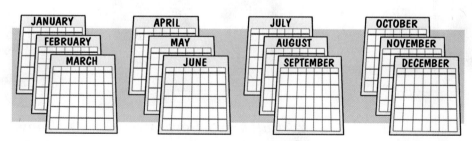

Seasons

spring

summer

fall/autumn

winter

What Are They Going to Do Tomorrow?

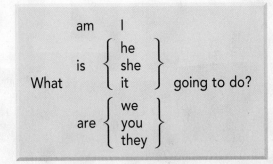

What
am { I }
is { he / she / it }
are { we / you / they }
going to do?

(I am) I'm
(He is) He's
(She is) She's
(It is) It's
(We are) We're
(You are) You're
(They are) They're
going to read.

A. What's Fred going to do tomorrow?

B. He's going to fix his car.

1. *Jenny?*

2. *Cathy and Dave?*

3. *Tony?*

4. *you and your brother?*

5. *Andrew?*

6. *Ashley?*

They're Going to the Beach

They're going (to go) to the beach.	=	They're going to the beach. They're going to go to the beach.
We're going (to go) swimming.	=	We're going swimming. We're going to go swimming.

today	*tomorrow*
this morning	tomorrow morning
this afternoon	tomorrow afternoon
this evening	tomorrow evening
tonight	tomorrow night

A. What are Mr. and Mrs. Brown going to do tomorrow?

B. They're going (to go) to the beach.

1. What's Anita going to do this morning?

2. What are Steve and Brenda going to do tonight?

3. What's Fernando going to do tomorrow evening?

4. What are you and your friends going to do tomorrow afternoon?

What are YOU going to do tomorrow?

129

When Are You Going to . . .?

Time Expressions

this _____
next _____
{
week / month / year
Sunday / Monday / Tuesday / Wednesday / Thursday / Friday / Saturday
January / February / March / April / May / June / July / August / September / October / November / December
spring / summer / fall (autumn) / winter
}

right now
right away
immediately
at once

When are you going to wash your clothes?

I'm going to wash them this week.

When are you going to fix our doorbell?

I'm going to fix it next Friday.

When are you going to cut your hair?

I'm going to cut it this summer.

When are you going to call the plumber?

I'm going to call him right now.

Practice conversations with other students. Use any of the time expressions on page 130.

1. When are you going to clean your garage?

2. When are you going to call your grandmother?

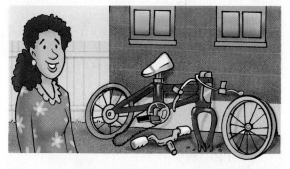

3. When are you going to fix your bicycle?

4. When are you going to visit us?

5. When are you going to wash your car?

6. When are you going to plant flowers this year?

7. When are you going to write to your Aunt Martha?

8. Mr. Smith! When are you going to iron those pants?

Now ask another student: "When are you going to _____?"

READING

HAPPY NEW YEAR!

It's December thirty-first, New Year's Eve. Ruth and Larry Carter are celebrating the holiday with their children, Nicole and Jonathan. The Carters are a very happy family this New Year's Eve. Next year is going to be a very good year for the entire family.

Next year, Ruth and Larry are going to take a long vacation. They're going to visit Larry's brother in Alaska. Nicole is going to finish high school. She's going to move to San Francisco and begin college. Jonathan is going to get his driver's license. He's going to save a lot of money and buy a used car.

As you can see, the Carters are really looking forward to next year. It's going to be a very happy year for all of them.

Happy New Year!

✔ READING CHECK-UP

COMPUTER CHAT

Fill in the missing words. Then practice this computer chat with another student.

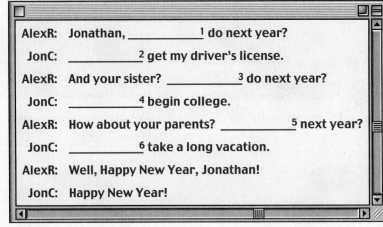

AlexR: Jonathan, _____ 1 do next year?

JonC: _____ 2 get my driver's license.

AlexR: And your sister? _____ 3 do next year?

JonC: _____ 4 begin college.

AlexR: How about your parents? _____ 5 next year?

JonC: _____ 6 take a long vacation.

AlexR: Well, Happy New Year, Jonathan!

JonC: Happy New Year!

LISTENING

Listen and choose the words you hear.

1. a. Tomorrow.
   b. This March.
2. a. Next December.
   b. Next November.
3. a. Next month.
   b. Next Monday.
4. a. This evening.
   b. This morning.
5. a. This summer.
   b. This Sunday.
6. a. This Tuesday.
   b. This Thursday.
7. a. This afternoon.
   b. Tomorrow afternoon.
8. a. Next year.
   b. Next week.
9. a. Next winter.
   b. Next summer.
10. a. This month.
    b. At once.

What's the Forecast?

| I We You They | want to | study. |
| He She It | wants to | |

A. What are you going to do tomorrow?

B. I don't know. I want to **go swimming**, but I think the weather is going to be bad.

A. Really? What's the forecast?

B. The radio says it's going to **rain**.

A. That's strange! According to the newspaper, it's going to **be sunny**.

B. I hope you're right. I REALLY want to **go swimming**.

1. *have a picnic*
rain
be nice

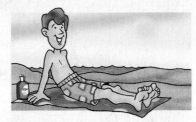

2. *go to the beach*
be cloudy
be sunny

3. *go sailing*
be foggy
be clear

4. *go skiing*
be warm
snow

5. *work in my garden*
be very hot
be cool

6. *take my children to the zoo*
be cold
be warm

Discuss in class: What's the weather today?
What's the weather forecast for tomorrow?

What Time Is It?

2:00

It's two o'clock.

2:15

It's two fifteen.
It's a quarter after two.

2:30

It's two thirty.
It's half past two.

2:45

It's two forty-five.
It's a quarter to three.

It's noon.
It's twelve noon.

It's midnight.
It's twelve midnight.

A. What time does the movie begin?

B. It begins at 8:00.

A. At 8:00?! Oh no! We're going to be late!

B. Why? What time is it?

A. It's 7:30! We have to leave RIGHT NOW!

B. I can't leave now. I'm SHAVING!

A. Please try to hurry! I don't want to be late for the movie.

A. What time does _____?

B. It _____ at _____.

A. At _____?! Oh no! We're going to be late!

B. Why? What time is it?

A. It's _____! We have to leave RIGHT NOW!

B. I can't leave now. I'm _____!

A. Please try to hurry! I don't want to be late for the _____.

1. What time does the football game begin?
3:00 / 2:30
taking a bath

2. What time does the bus leave?
7:15 / 6:45
packing my suitcase

3. What time does the train leave?
5:30 / 5:15
taking a shower

4. What time does the concert begin?
8:00 / 7:45
looking for my pants

How to Say It!

Asking the Time

A. { What time is it?
{ What's the time?

B. It's 4:00.

A. { Can you tell me the time?
{ Do you know the time?

B. Yes. It's 4:00.

Practice conversations with other students. Ask the time in different ways.

THE FORTUNE TELLER

Walter is visiting Madame Sophia, the famous fortune teller. He's wondering about his future, and Madame Sophia is telling him what is going to happen next year. According to Madame Sophia, next year is going to be a very interesting year in Walter's life.

In January he's going to meet a very nice woman and fall in love.

In February he's going to get married.

In March he's going to take a trip to a warm, sunny place.

In April he's going to have a bad cold.

In May his parents are going to move to a beautiful city in California.

In June there's going to be a fire in his apartment building, and he's going to have to find a new place to live.

In July his friends are going to give him a DVD player for his birthday.

In August his boss is going to fire him.

In September he's going to start a new job with a very big salary.

In October he's going to be in a car accident, but he isn't going to be hurt.

In November he's going to be on a television game show and win a million dollars.

And in December he's going to become a father!

According to Madame Sophia, a lot is going to happen in Walter's life next year. But Walter isn't sure he believes any of this. He doesn't believe in fortunes or fortune tellers. But in January he's going to get a haircut and buy a lot of new clothes, just in case Madame Sophia is right and he meets a wonderful woman and falls in love!

✔ READING *CHECK-UP*

Q & A

Walter is talking to Madame Sophia. Using these models, create dialogs based on the story.

A. Tell me, what's going to happen in *January*?
B. In *January*? Oh! *January* is going to be a very good month!
A. Really? What's going to happen?
B. *You're going to meet a very nice woman and fall in love.*
A. Oh! That's wonderful!

A. Tell me, what's going to happen in *April*?
B. In *April*? Oh! *April* is going to be a very bad month!
A. Really? What's going to happen?
B. *You're going to have a bad cold.*
A. Oh! That's terrible!

PRONUNCIATION *Going to & Want to*

> going to = gonna
> want to = wanna

Listen. Then say it.

I'm going to study.

It's going to rain.

We want to go swimming.

They want to leave.

Say it. Then listen.

He's going to cook.

They're going to paint.

I want to read.

We want to go to the beach.

SIDE by SIDE JOURNAL

What are you going to do tomorrow? Write about it in your journal.

FUTURE: GOING TO

	am	I	
What	is	he she it	going to do?
	are	we you they	

(I am)	I'm	
(He is) (She is) (It is)	He's She's It's	going to read.
(We are) (You are) (They are)	We're You're They're	

Complete the sentences using *going to* and the correct verb.

go	read	wash	watch	write

1. A. What's your husband going to do this afternoon?

B. _____ _____ _____ _____ a book.

2. A. What are you going to do this morning?

B. _____ _____ _____ _____ a letter to my aunt.

3. A. What are Sally and Paul going to do tonight?

B. _____ _____ _____ _____ TV.

4. A. What are you and your wife going to do this Saturday?

B. _____ _____ _____ _____ our windows.

5. A. What's your sister going to do this Sunday?

B. _____ _____ _____ _____ to the beach.

TIME EXPRESSIONS

I'm going to call	today. this morning. this afternoon. this evening. tonight.	tomorrow. tomorrow morning. tomorrow afternoon. tomorrow evening. tomorrow night.	right now. right away. immediately. at once.

I'm going to fix my car	this next	week / month / year. Sunday / Monday / Tuesday / . . . / Saturday. January / February / March / . . . / December. spring / summer / fall (autumn) / winter.

Number the following from the present (1) to the future (12).

____ next Saturday
____ tomorrow afternoon
____ next year
____ this Friday
_1_ immediately
____ this Wednesday
____ next month
____ tomorrow night
____ tonight
____ this evening
____ next Tuesday
____ this afternoon

It's	eleven o'clock.		11:00
	eleven fifteen.	a quarter after eleven.	11:15
	eleven thirty.	half past eleven.	11:30
	eleven forty-five.	a quarter to twelve.	11:45

Match the times.

____ **1.** 3:15   **a.** three forty-five

____ **2.** 2:45   **b.** half past two

____ **3.** 2:30   **c.** a quarter after three

____ **4.** 3:45   **d.** a quarter to three

WANT TO

I We You They	want to	
		study.
He She It	wants to	

Choose the correct word.

1. I (want to wants to) go to a movie tomorrow night.

2. My husband (want to wants to) go to the beach tomorrow.

3. My sister and I (want to wants to) go swimming today.

4. My parents (want to wants to) buy a new car.

5. Do you (want to wants to) have a picnic this afternoon?

6. My grandmother (want to wants to) work in her garden today.

Time Zones

What time is it right now? What time is it in other parts of the world? How do you know?

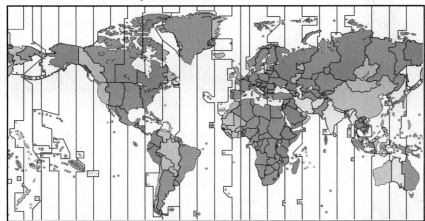

There are 24 time zones around the world. In each time zone, it is a different hour of the day. The time zone that is east of your time zone is one hour ahead. The time zone to your west is one hour behind. So, for example, when it's 10:00 in Chicago, it's 11:00 in New York, it's 9:00 in Denver, and it's 8:00 in Los Angeles.

New Zealand is 12 time zones to the east of London. Therefore, when it's midnight in London and people are sleeping, it's noon the next day in New Zealand and people are eating lunch!

FACT FILE

A Moment in the Life of the World

TIME AND DAY	PLACE
5:00 A.M.* Monday morning	Los Angeles, USA
7:00 A.M. Monday morning	Mexico City, Mexico
8:00 A.M. Monday morning	New York City, USA; Toronto, Canada
9:00 A.M. Monday morning	Caracas, Venezuela
10:00 A.M. Monday morning	Rio de Janeiro, Brazil; Buenos Aires, Argentina
1:00 P.M.* Monday afternoon	London, England; Lisbon, Portugal
2:00 P.M. Monday afternoon	Paris, France; Madrid, Spain; Rome, Italy
3:00 P.M. Monday afternoon	Athens, Greece; Istanbul, Turkey
4:00 P.M. Monday afternoon	Moscow, Russia
9:00 P.M. Monday night	Hong Kong, China
10:00 P.M. Monday night	Seoul, Korea; Tokyo, Japan
12:00 A.M. Tuesday morning	Sydney, Australia

*A.M. = 12:00 midnight to 11:59 in the morning   P.M. = 12:00 noon to 11:59 at night

BUILD YOUR VOCABULARY!

Occupations

A. **What do you do?**
B. **I'm a/an _____ .**

 ■ architect

 ■ carpenter

 ■ cashier

 ■ farmer

 ■ lawyer

 ■ painter

 ■ pilot

 ■ translator

 ■ waiter

 ■ waitress

AROUND THE WORLD

Time and Culture

People in different cultures think of time in different ways.

In your culture, do people arrive on time for work? Do people arrive on time for appointments? Do people arrive on time for parties? Tell about time in your culture.

LISTENING

Thank You for Calling the Multiplex Cinema!

_c_ **1**

___ **2**

___ **3**

___ **4**

___ **5**

a. _The Fortune Teller_

b. _Tomorrow Is Right Now_

c. _The Spanish Dancer_

d. _The Time Zone Machine_

e. _When Are You Going to Call the Plumber?_

Global Exchange

JulieP: I'm going to be very busy this weekend. On Friday evening, I'm going to get together with my friends from college. We're going to have dinner, and then we're going to a concert. On Saturday morning, I have to clean my apartment because my parents are going to visit me in the afternoon. In the evening, we're going to go bowling. On Sunday I'm going to teach my Sunday school class in the morning, I'm going to a soccer game in the afternoon, and I'm going to wash my clothes in the evening. How about you? What are you going to do this weekend?

Send a message to a keypal. Tell about your plans for the weekend.

What Are They Saying?

Past Tense:
Regular Verbs
Introduction to Irregular Verbs

- **Past Actions and Activities**
- **Ailments**
- **Describing an Event**
- **Making a Doctor's Appointment**

VOCABULARY PREVIEW

1. headache
2. stomachache
3. toothache
4. backache
5. earache
6. cold
7. fever
8. cough
9. sore throat

How Do You Feel Today?

A. How do you feel today?

B. Not so good.

A. What's the matter?

B. I have a headache.

A. I'm sorry to hear that.

1. *stomachache*

2. *toothache*

3. *backache*

4. *earache*

5. *cold*

6. *fever*

7. *cough*

8. *sore throat*

How to Say It!

Saying How You Feel

How do you feel today?

I feel great! I feel fine. I feel okay.

I'm glad to hear that.

How do you feel today?

So-so. Not so good. I feel terrible.

I'm sorry to hear that.

Practice conversations with other students.

What Did You Do Yesterday?

I work every day.
I worked yesterday.

I play the piano every day.
I played the piano yesterday.

I rest every day.
I rested yesterday.

What did you do yesterday?

I worked.

1. cook

2. wash my car

3. fix my bicycle

4. brush my teeth

5. watch TV

6. type*

7. dance*

8. bake*

9. clean

10. play the piano

11. yawn

12. listen to music

13. shave*

14. smile*

15. cry†

16. study†

17. shout

18. rest

19. plant flowers

20. wait for the bus

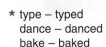

* type – typed
  dance – danced
  bake – baked

shave – shaved
smile – smiled

† cry – cried
  study – studied

143

What's the Matter?

I / We / You / They	work every day.
He / She / It	works every day.

I / We / You / They / He / She / It	worked yesterday.

A. How does David feel?

B. Not so good.

A. What's the matter?

B. He has a backache.

A. A backache? How did he get it?

B. He played basketball all day.*

* Or: all morning / all afternoon / all evening / all night

1. *Brian*

2. *Linda*

3. *you*

4. *Gary*

5. *Maria*

6. *Charlie*

7. *Mrs. Clark*

8. *you*

9. *Carlos*

| eat – ate | sing – sang | drink – drank | sit – sat | ride – rode |

10. *Daniel*

11. *Jennifer*

12. *you*

13. *Sarah*

14. *you*

15. *Tim*

ROLE PLAY *Do You Want to Make an Appointment?*

You don't feel very well today. Call the doctor's office and make an appointment.

A. Doctor's Office.

B. Hello. This is _____.

A. Hello, Mr./Ms./Mrs. _____.
How are you?

B. Not so good.

A. I'm sorry to hear that. What seems to be
the problem?

B. I _____ all _____ yesterday,
and now I have a TERRIBLE _____.

A. I see. Do you want to make an
appointment?

B. Yes, please.

A. Can you come in tomorrow at
_____ o'clock?

B. At _____ o'clock? Yes. That's fine.
Thank you.

THE WILSONS' PARTY

Mr. and Mrs. Wilson invited all their friends and neighbors to a party last night. They stayed home all day yesterday and prepared for the party.

In the morning the Wilsons worked outside. Their daughter, Margaret, cleaned the yard. Their son, Bob, painted the fence. Mrs. Wilson planted flowers in the garden, and Mr. Wilson fixed their broken front steps.

In the afternoon the Wilsons worked inside the house. Margaret washed the floors and vacuumed the living room carpet. Bob dusted the furniture and cleaned the basement. Mr. and Mrs. Wilson stayed in the kitchen all afternoon. He cooked spaghetti for dinner, and she baked apple pies for dessert.

The Wilsons finished all their work at six o'clock. Their house looked beautiful inside and out!

The Wilsons' guests arrived at about 7:30. After they arrived, they all sat in the living room. They ate cheese and crackers, drank lemonade, and talked. Some people talked about their children. Other people talked about the weather. And EVERYBODY talked about how beautiful the Wilsons' house looked inside and out!

The Wilsons served dinner in the dining room at 9:00. Everybody enjoyed the meal very much. They liked Mr. Wilson's spaghetti and they "loved" Mrs. Wilson's apple pie. In fact, everybody asked for seconds.

After dinner everybody sat in the living room again. First, Bob Wilson played the piano and his sister, Margaret, sang. Then, Mr. and Mrs. Wilson showed a video of their trip to Hawaii. After that, they turned on the music and everybody danced.

As you can see, the Wilsons' guests enjoyed the party very much. In fact, nobody wanted to go home!

✔ READING *CHECK-UP*

WHAT'S THE ANSWER?

1. What did Margaret and Bob Wilson do in the morning?
2. How did Mr. and Mrs. Wilson prepare for the party in the afternoon?
3. When did the guests arrive?
4. Where did the guests sit after they arrived?
5. What did they eat and drink before dinner?
6. What did Margaret do after dinner?
7. What did Mr. and Mrs. Wilson do after dinner?

LISTENING

Listen and choose the word you hear.

1. a. plant   b. planted
2. a. work   b. worked
3. a. study   b. studied
4. a. sit   b. sat
5. a. drink   b. drank
6. a. wait   b. waited

7. a. finish   b. finished
8. a. invite   b. invited
9. a. eat   b. ate
10. a. clean   b. cleaned
11. a. wash   b. washed
12. a. watch   b. watched

IN YOUR OWN WORDS

FOR WRITING OR DISCUSSION

A PARTY

Tell about a party you enjoyed.

What did you eat?
What did you drink?
What did people do at the party?
    (eat, dance, talk about . . .)

PRONUNCIATION   *Past Tense Endings*

Put these words in the correct column. Then practice saying the words in each column.

| cleaned | danced | dusted | painted | played | studied | talked | typed | waited |

{t}

_____

_____

_____

{d}

cleaned

_____

_____

{ɪd}

_____

_____

_____

Listen. Then say it.

I cooked, I cleaned, and I dusted.

I worked, I played, and I planted flowers.

Say it. Then listen.

I typed, I studied, and I painted.

I talked, I cried, and I shouted.

**What did you eat yesterday?
What did you drink?
Write about it in your journal.**

GRAMMAR FOCUS

PAST TENSE

| I He She It We You They | worked yesterday. |

[t]	I work**ed**. I dan**ced**.
[d]	I clean**ed**. I play**ed**.
[ɪd]	I rest**ed**. I shout**ed**.

IRREGULAR VERBS

eat – ate
drink – drank
ride – rode
sing – sang
sit – sat

Complete each sentence with the past tense of the correct verb.

| drink | listen | play | sing | study | wash |
| eat | plant | ride | sit | wait | watch |

1. I _____ my car yesterday.

2. I _____ TV yesterday.

3. I _____ the piano yesterday.

4. I _____ to music yesterday.

5. I _____ flowers yesterday.

6. I _____ English yesterday.

7. I _____ four cookies this afternoon.

8. I _____ milk with my lunch today.

9. I have a sore throat because I _____ all day yesterday.

10. My daughter _____ her bicycle all afternoon.

11. I _____ at my desk all day yesterday.

12. I _____ for the bus all morning.

Past Tense:
Yes/No Questions
Short Answers
Time Expressions
WH-Questions
More Irregular Verbs

- Reporting Past Actions and Activities
- Giving Reasons
- Giving Excuses

VOCABULARY PREVIEW

1. got up
2. took a shower
3. had breakfast
4. read the newspaper
5. did exercises
6. ate lunch
7. drove to the supermarket
8. bought groceries
9. made dinner
10. wrote a letter
11. saw a movie
12. went to sleep

I Brushed My Teeth

I worked.
I didn't work.
(did not)

Did you work?
Yes, I did.
No, I didn't.

today	yesterday
this morning	yesterday morning
this afternoon	yesterday afternoon
this evening	yesterday evening
tonight	last night

Did you brush your hair this morning?

No, I didn't. I brushed my teeth.

1. Did he wash his windows yesterday morning?

2. Did she paint her kitchen this afternoon?

3. Did they study English last night?

4. Did you and your friends play tennis yesterday afternoon?

5. Did he bake a pie today?

6. Did you listen to the news this morning?

We Went to the Supermarket

go
went

1. Did you take the subway this morning?

take
took

2. Did he have a headache last night?

have
had

3. Did Wanda get up at 9:00 this morning?

get
got

4. Did your children make dinner today?

make
made

5. Did Michael buy a car yesterday?

buy
bought

6. Did they do their homework last night?

do
did

7. Did Tommy write to his girlfriend this week?

write
wrote

8. Did you read the newspaper this afternoon?

read
read

TALK ABOUT IT! *What Did They Do Yesterday?*

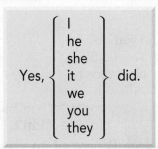

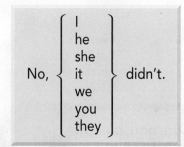

Betty fixed her car yesterday morning.
She washed her windows yesterday afternoon.
She listened to music last night.

Bob read the newspaper yesterday morning.
He went to the library yesterday afternoon.
He wrote letters last night.

Nick and Nancy went to the supermarket
   yesterday morning.
They bought a new car yesterday afternoon.
They cleaned their apartment last night.

Jennifer did her exercises yesterday
   morning.
She planted flowers yesterday afternoon.
She took a bath last night.

Using these models, talk about the people above with other students in your class.

A. Did *Betty fix her car yesterday morning?*

B. Yes, *she* did.

A. Did *Bob go to the library last night?*

B. No, *he* didn't. *He went to the library yesterday afternoon.*

How About You?

What did you do yesterday morning?
What did you do yesterday afternoon?
What did you do last night?

Giving an Excuse

A. I'm sorry I'm late. *I missed the bus.*
B. I see.

Practice the interactions on this page.
Apologize and give excuses.

INTERACTIONS

A. I'm sorry I'm late. _____.
B. I see.

I missed the _____.
(bus / train . . .)

I had a _____ this morning.
(headache / stomachache / . . .)

I had to go to the _____.
(doctor / dentist / . . .)

I forgot* my _____ and had to
go back home and get it.
(briefcase / backpack / . . .)

A thief stole* my _____.
(bicycle / car / . . .)

THINK ABOUT IT! *Good Excuses & Bad Excuses*

The people above have good excuses. Here are some BAD excuses:

I got up late.

I had a big breakfast today.

I met* a friend on the way to work / school.

Discuss with other students: What are some good excuses? What are some bad
excuses? Why are these excuses good or bad?

* forget – forgot   steal – stole   meet – met

READING

LATE FOR WORK

Victor usually gets up at 7 A.M. He does his morning exercises for twenty minutes, he takes a long shower, he has a big breakfast, and he leaves for work at 8:00. He usually drives his car to work and gets there at 8:30.

This morning, however, he didn't get up at 7 A.M. He got up at 6:30. He didn't do his morning exercises for twenty minutes. He did them for only five minutes. He didn't take a long shower. He took a very quick shower. He didn't have a big breakfast. He had a very small breakfast. He didn't leave for work at 8:00. He left for work at 7:00.

Victor didn't drive his car to work this morning. He drove it to the repair shop. Then he walked a mile to the train station, and he waited for the train for fifteen minutes. After he got off the train, he walked half a mile to his office.

Even though Victor got up early and rushed out of the house this morning, he didn't get to work on time. He got there forty-five minutes late. When his supervisor saw him, she got angry and she shouted at him for five minutes. Poor Victor! He really tried to get to work on time this morning.

READING *CHECK-UP*

WHAT'S THE ANSWER?

1. Did Victor get up at 7 A.M. today?
2. What time did he get up?
3. Did he leave for work at 8:00 this morning?
4. What time did he leave for work?
5. Did he drive his car to the repair shop today?

6. How did he get to the train station?
7. Did Victor get to work on time?
8. Did his supervisor get angry at him?
9. What did she do?

1. Victor (got up   didn't get up) at 6:30 A.M. this morning.
2. He (did   didn't do) his exercises for twenty minutes today.
3. He (took   didn't take) a very quick shower this morning.
4. He (left   didn't leave) for work at 8:00 this morning.
5. He (took   didn't take) the train to work today.
6. He (got   didn't get) to work on time this morning.

LISTENING

Listen and put a check next to all the things these people did today.

Carla's Day
___ got up early
___ got up late
___ took a bath
___ took a shower
___ had breakfast
___ had lunch
___ took the subway
___ took the bus
___ met her brother
___ met her mother
___ had dinner
___ made dinner
___ saw a movie
___ saw a play

Brian's Day
___ fixed his car
___ fixed his bicycle
___ cleaned his garage
___ cleaned his yard
___ painted his bedroom
___ planted flowers
___ washed his windows
___ watched TV
___ read the newspaper
___ read a magazine
___ rode his bicycle
___ wrote to his brother
___ took a shower
___ took a bath

COMPLETE THE STORY

Complete the story with the correct forms of the verbs.

| buy | eat | get | go | make | see | sit | take |

SHIRLEY'S DAY OFF

Shirley enjoyed her day off yesterday. She
_____¹ up late, _____² jogging in the park,
_____³ a long shower, and _____⁴ a big breakfast.
In the afternoon, she _____⁵ a movie with her sister.
Then she _____⁶ groceries at the supermarket, and
she _____⁷ a big dinner for her parents. After dinner,
Shirley and her parents _____⁸ in the living room and
talked. Shirley had a very nice day off yesterday.

How About You?

Tell about a day off YOU
enjoyed. What did you
do in the morning?
in the afternoon?
in the evening?

PRONUNCIATION *Did you*

Listen. Then say it.

Did you go to the bank?

Did you brush your hair?

Did you listen to the news?

Did you take the subway?

Say it. Then listen.

Did you go to the supermarket?

Did you play tennis?

Did you read the newspaper?

Did you see a movie?

SIDE by SIDE JOURNAL

What did you do yesterday? Write in your journal about all the things you did.

GRAMMAR FOCUS

PAST TENSE: YES/NO QUESTIONS

Did	I he she it we you they	work?

SHORT ANSWERS

Yes,	I he she it we you they	did.

No,	I he she it we you they	didn't.

PAST TENSE: WH-QUESTIONS

What did	I he she it we you they	do?

TIME EXPRESSIONS

Did you study English	yesterday? yesterday morning? yesterday afternoon? yesterday evening? last night?

Complete the conversations with the correct forms of these verbs.

do   go   have   listen   study   take   wash   watch

1. A. Did you _____ the bus this morning?
   B. No, I didn't. I _____ the train.

2. A. Did your children _____ last night?
   B. Yes, they did. They _____ English.

3. A. Did you _____ your windows yesterday?
   B. No, we didn't. We _____ our car.

4. A. Did you _____ to the bank this morning?
   B. No, I didn't. I _____ to the post office.

5. A. Did you _____ a stomachache yesterday?
   B. Yes, I _____. I also _____ a headache.

6. A. _____ Stella _____ TV last night?
   B. No, she didn't. She _____ to music.

17

To Be: Past Tense

- Television Commercials
- Describing Physical States and Emotions
- Telling About the Past
- Biographies and Autobiographies

VOCABULARY PREVIEW

 1

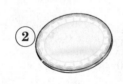 2

 3

 4

 5

 6

 7

 8

 9

1. sad – happy
2. clean – dirty
3. heavy – thin

4. hungry – full
5. sick – healthy
6. tiny – enormous

7. dull – shiny
8. comfortable – uncomfortable
9. tired – energetic

PRESTO Commercials

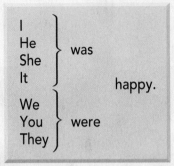

I
He
She
It
} was

happy.

We
You
They
} were

Before our family bought PRESTO Vitamins, we were always tired.
I was tired.
My wife was tired.
My children were tired, too.
Now we're energetic, because WE bought PRESTO Vitamins. How about you?

Before our family bought _____, we were always _____.

    I was _____.

    My wife/husband was _____.

    My children were _____, too.

Now we're _____ because WE bought _____. How about you?

Using the above script, prepare commercials for these other fine PRESTO products.

1. *sad*   *happy*

2. *hungry*   *full*

3. *dirty*   *clean*

4. *sick*   *healthy*

5. *heavy*   *thin*

6. _____   _____

Before I Bought PRESTO Shampoo

Before I bought PRESTO Shampoo, my hair **was** always dirty. Now **it's** clean!

1. Before we bought PRESTO Toothpaste, our teeth _____ yellow. Now _____ white!

2. Before we bought PRESTO Paint, our house _____ ugly. Now _____ beautiful!

3. Before I bought a PRESTO armchair, I _____ uncomfortable. Now _____ very comfortable!

4. Before we bought PRESTO Dog Food, our dog _____ tiny. Now _____ enormous!

5. Before I bought PRESTO Window Cleaner, my windows _____ dirty. Now _____ clean!

6. Before we bought PRESTO Floor Wax, our kitchen floor _____ dull. Now _____ shiny!

How to Say It!

Recommending Products

A. Can you recommend a good *toothpaste*?

B. Yes. I recommend *PRESTO Toothpaste*. It's very good.

A. Thanks for the recommendation.

Practice conversations with other students. Make recommendations about real products.

Were You at the Ballgame Last Night?

I		
He		wasn't
She		(was not)
It		
We		weren't
You		(were not)
They		

A. Were you at the ballgame last night?

B. No, I wasn't. I was at the movies.

1. Was Albert happy yesterday?

2. Were they at home this morning?

3. Was it cold yesterday?

4. Was your grandfather a doctor?

5. Was I a quiet baby?

6. Were you at home last weekend?

7. Was Gloria on time for her plane?

8. Were your children late for the school bus?

9. Was the food good at the restaurant?

Did You Sleep Well Last Night?

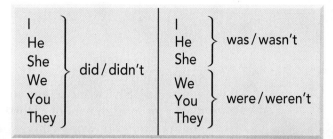

I He She We You They	did / didn't	I He She	was / wasn't	
		We You They	were / weren't	

A. Did you sleep well last night?
B. Yes, I did. I was tired.

A. Did Roger sleep well last night?
B. No, he didn't. He wasn't tired.

1. Did Frank have a big breakfast today?
   Yes, _____. _____ hungry.

2. Did Thelma have a big breakfast today?
   No, _____. _____ hungry.

3. Did Mr. Chen go to the doctor yesterday?
   Yes, _____. _____ sick.

4. Did Mrs. Chen go to the doctor yesterday?
   No, _____. _____ sick.

5. Did Billy finish his milk?
   Yes, _____. _____ thirsty.

6. Did Katie finish her milk?
   No, _____. _____ thirsty.

7. Did Sonia miss the train?
   Yes, _____. _____ late.

8. Did Stuart miss the train?
   No , _____. _____ late.

READING

MARIA GOMEZ

Maria Gomez was born in Peru. She grew* up in a small village. She began* school when she was six years old. She went to elementary school, but she didn't go to high school. Her family was very poor, and she had to go to work when she was thirteen years old. She worked on an assembly line in a shoe factory.

When Maria was seventeen years old, her family moved to the United States. First they lived in Los Angeles, and then they moved to San Francisco. When Maria arrived in the United States, she wasn't very happy. She missed her friends back in Peru, and she didn't speak one word of English. She began to study English at night, and she worked in a factory during the day.

Maria studied very hard. She learned English, and she got a good job as a secretary. Maria still studies at night, but now she studies advertising at a business school. She wants to work for an advertising company some day and write commercials.

Maria still misses her friends back home, but she communicates with them very often over the Internet. She's very happy now, and she's looking forward to an exciting future.

✔ READING CHECK-UP

WHAT'S THE ANSWER?

1. Where was Maria born?
2. Did she grow up in a large city?
3. When did she begin school?
4. What happened when Maria was seventeen years old?
5. Why was Maria unhappy when she arrived in the United States?
6. What is Maria's occupation?
7. What does she want to do in the future?
8. How does Maria communicate with her friends back home?

* grow – grew   begin – began

WHAT'S THE ORDER?

Put these sentences in the correct order based on the story.

____ Maria's family moved to the United States.
____ Maria studies advertising now.
_1_ Maria grew up in a small village.
____ Maria's family moved to San Francisco.
____ Maria worked in a shoe factory.
____ Maria began to study English at night.
____ Maria went to elementary school.
____ Maria's family lived in Los Angeles.
____ Maria got a job as a secretary.

LISTENING

Listen and choose the correct answer.

1. a. They were sick.
   b. They're sick now.
2. a. Their old chairs were comfortable.
   b. Their new chairs are comfortable.
3. a. Lucy was very thirsty.
   b. Lucy wasn't thirsty.
4. a. Fred was on time this morning.
   b. Fred wasn't on time this morning.
5. a. Peter and Mary were at work yesterday.
   b. Peter and Mary are at work today.
6. a. Their kitchen floor wasn't shiny.
   b. Their kitchen floor is dull now.

Autobiography

Tell a story about yourself. In your story, answer questions such as:

Where were you born?
Where did you grow up?
Where did you go to school?
What did you study?
When did you move? Where?

ON YOUR OWN *Do You Remember Your Childhood?*

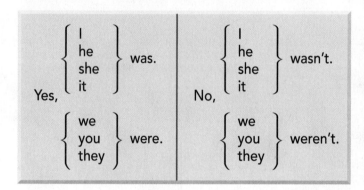

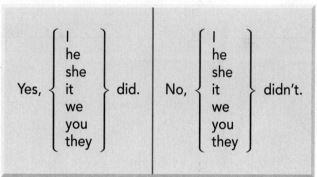

Answer these questions and then ask other students in your class.

1. What did you look like?
   Were you tall? thin? pretty? handsome? cute?
   Did you have curly hair? straight hair? long hair?
   Did you have dimples? freckles?

2. Did you have many friends?
   What did you do with your friends?
   What games did you play?

3. Did you like school?
   Who was your favorite teacher? Why?
   What was your favorite subject? Why?

4. What did you do in your spare time?
   Did you have a hobby?
   Did you play sports?

5. Who was your favorite hero?

163

PRONUNCIATION Intonation of Yes/No Questions and WH-Questions

Listen. Then say it.

Were you tall?

Did you have long hair?

What did you look like?

Who was your favorite teacher?

Say it. Then listen.

Were you short?

Did you have freckles?

Where did you grow up?

When did you move?

SIDE *by* **SIDE JOURNAL**

Write in your journal about your childhood. What did you look like? What did you do with your friends? Did you like school? What did you do in your spare time?

GRAMMAR FOCUS

To Be: Past Tense

I He She It	was	
We You They	were	happy.

I He She It	wasn't	
We You They	weren't	tired.

Was	I he she it	
Were	we you they	late?

Yes,	I he she it	was.
	we you they	were.

No,	I he she it	wasn't.
	we you they	weren't.

Complete the sentences.

1. A. _____ it hot yesterday?
   B. Yes, it _____. It _____ very hot.

2. A. _____ you at home yesterday evening?
   B. No, we _____. We _____ at the movies.

3. A. _____ George on time for work today?
   B. No, he _____. He _____ late.

4. A. _____ your neighbors noisy last night?
   B. Yes, they _____. They _____ very noisy all night.

5. A. _____ your wife at the ballgame last night?
   B. Yes, _____ _____. She _____ next to me.

6. A. _____ you at work last night?
   B. No, _____ _____. I _____ at the laundromat.

7. A. _____ your homework difficult today?
   B. No, _____ _____. It _____ very easy.

8. A. _____ I a healthy baby?
   B. Yes, _____ _____. You _____ a very healthy baby.

Volume 1   Number 7

Advertisements

How do advertisers sell their products?

Advertisements are everywhere! They are on television, on the radio, and in newspapers and magazines. Ads are also on billboards, on buses and trains, and even in movie theaters. People get advertisements in their mail. There are also a lot of advertisements on the Internet.

Advertisements are sometimes in unusual places—in elevators, on top of taxis, and in public bathrooms. People sometimes carry signs with ads on the street, and small airplanes sometimes carry signs in the sky. Advertisers are always looking for new places for their ads.

FACT FILE

Countries Where Advertisers Spend the Most Money	
United States	Brazil
Japan	Italy
United Kingdom	Australia
Germany	Canada
France	Korea

LISTENING

And Now a Word From Our Sponsors!

And Now a Word From Our Sponsors!

_d_	**1** Dazzle	**a.**	floor wax
____	**2** Shiny-Time	**b.**	dog shampoo
____	**3** Energy Plus	**c.**	throat lozenges
____	**4** Lucky Lemon Drops	**d.**	toothpaste
____	**5** K-9 Shine	**e.**	vitamins

BUILD YOUR VOCABULARY!

Opposites

  dark   light

 fancy   plain

 fast   slow

 good   bad

 heavy   light

 high   low

 long   short

 neat   messy

 open   closed

wet   dry

165

Shopping

People around the world buy things in different ways.

This person is shopping in a store.

These people are buying things at an outdoor market.

This person is ordering something from a catalog over the telephone.

This person is buying something from a home shopping channel on TV.

These people are looking for things at a yard sale.

This person is shopping on the Internet.

What are the ways people buy things in different countries you know?

Global Exchange

TedG: I had a very busy day today. I got up at 6:30, took a shower, ate breakfast, and went to school. In my English class this morning, I read a long story, and I wrote my autobiography. I didn't have time for lunch because I had to meet with my Spanish teacher. After I met with her, I went to math class. We had a big test today. It was very difficult! After school, I went to a basketball game. Then I went home, did some homework, had dinner, and did some more homework. How about you? What did you do today?

Send a message to a keypal. Tell about what you did today.

What Are They Saying?

Choose the correct answer.

1. My _____ is David Soto.
   - Ⓐ address
   - Ⓑ telephone
   - Ⓒ name
   - Ⓓ fax

2. My _____ number is 947-2681.
   - Ⓐ apartment
   - Ⓑ e-mail
   - Ⓒ address
   - Ⓓ phone

3. I'm _____.
   - Ⓐ Susan Black
   - Ⓑ Main Street
   - Ⓒ San Francisco
   - Ⓓ my name

4. Where _____ you from?
   - Ⓐ is
   - Ⓑ are
   - Ⓒ am
   - Ⓓ I'm

5. What's your apartment _____?
   - Ⓐ name
   - Ⓑ number
   - Ⓒ license
   - Ⓓ e-mail

6. _____ do you spell that?
   - Ⓐ What's
   - Ⓑ Hi
   - Ⓒ How
   - Ⓓ Where

7. My _____ name is Peter.
   - Ⓐ phone
   - Ⓑ address
   - Ⓒ apartment
   - Ⓓ first

8. My e-mail address is _____.
   - Ⓐ Florida
   - Ⓑ Bob@worldnet.com
   - Ⓒ 634 Main Street
   - Ⓓ Miller

9. My _____ number is 395RBN.
   - Ⓐ license
   - Ⓑ address
   - Ⓒ telephone
   - Ⓓ alphabet

10. Nice to _____ you.
    - Ⓐ name
    - Ⓑ spell
    - Ⓒ meet
    - Ⓓ number

SKILLS CHECK

Match the "can do" statement and the correct sentence.

_____ 1. I can say my name.

_____ 2. I can spell my name.

_____ 3. I can greet people.

_____ 4. I can give my address.

_____ 5. I can give my telephone number.

_____ 6. I can give my e-mail address.

_____ 7. I can tell where I'm from.

_____ 8. I can say the alphabet.

a. Mexico City.

b. (213) 765-4218.

c. omar42@zmail.com.

d. A-B-C . . . X-Y-Z.

e. My name is Omar.

f. 197 Main Street.

g. O-M-A-R.

h. Nice to meet you.

Choose the correct answer.

1. A. Where's the book?
   B. ____ on the desk.
   Ⓐ He's
   Ⓑ It's
   Ⓒ She's
   Ⓓ They're

2. Where ____ you?
   Ⓐ is
   Ⓑ am
   Ⓒ are
   Ⓓ from

3. A. Where are Mr. and Mrs. Lee?
   B. ____ in the kitchen.
   Ⓐ They're
   Ⓑ We're
   Ⓒ She's
   Ⓓ He's

4. A. ____ Mrs. Lopez?
   B. She's in the living room.
   Ⓐ Where
   Ⓑ What's
   Ⓒ Where's
   Ⓓ How

5. The computer is ____ the table.
   Ⓐ in
   Ⓑ it
   Ⓒ from
   Ⓓ on

6. A. Where's the ____?
   B. It's in the classroom.
   Ⓐ garage
   Ⓑ globe
   Ⓒ park
   Ⓓ yard

7. Where's my cell ____?
   Ⓐ room
   Ⓑ book
   Ⓒ phone
   Ⓓ class

8. A. Where's George?
   B. He's in the ____.
   Ⓐ table
   Ⓑ telephone
   Ⓒ map
   Ⓓ hospital

9. A. Where's the ____?
   B. It's on the wall.
   Ⓐ basement
   Ⓑ bulletin board
   Ⓒ car
   Ⓓ park

10. Manuel is from ____.
    Ⓐ Puerto Rico
    Ⓑ Mexican
    Ⓒ Puerto Rican
    Ⓓ English

SKILLS CHECK

Match the "can do" statement and the correct sentence.

____ 1. I can ask the location of objects.

____ 2. I can give the location of objects.

____ 3. I can give my location.

____ 4. I can ask a person's location.

____ 5. I can give my nationality.

____ 6. I can tell where I'm from.

____ 7. I can ask where a person is from.

____ 8. I can greet people.

a. Where are you?

b. Where are you from?

c. Hi. How are you?

d. The ruler is on the desk.

e. I'm from Tokyo.

f. I'm Mexican.

g. Where's the dictionary?

h. I'm in the kitchen.

Choose the correct answer.

1. A. What are you doing?
   B. _____ watching TV.
   Ⓐ He's
   Ⓑ They're
   Ⓒ We're
   Ⓓ You're

2. A. Where's Ms. Williams?
   B. _____ in the park.
   Ⓐ I'm
   Ⓑ He's
   Ⓒ They're
   Ⓓ She's

3. A. _____ they doing?
   B. They're reading.
   Ⓐ What's
   Ⓑ What are
   Ⓒ Where are
   Ⓓ Where's

4. A. _____ Mr. and Mrs. Lee?
   B. They're in the yard.
   Ⓐ Where are
   Ⓑ What are
   Ⓒ Where's
   Ⓓ What's

5. Carla _____ reading the newspaper.
   Ⓐ in
   Ⓑ it
   Ⓒ is
   Ⓓ are

6. We're studying _____.
   Ⓐ cards
   Ⓑ TV
   Ⓒ lunch
   Ⓓ English

7. He's _____ the piano.
   Ⓐ playing
   Ⓑ sleeping
   Ⓒ drinking
   Ⓓ cooking

8. He's _____ dinner.
   Ⓐ studying
   Ⓑ reading
   Ⓒ eating
   Ⓓ playing

9. They're drinking _____.
   Ⓐ the guitar
   Ⓑ cards
   Ⓒ milk
   Ⓓ the car

10. He's _____ music.
    Ⓐ eating
    Ⓑ listening to
    Ⓒ cooking
    Ⓓ sleeping

SKILLS CHECK

Match the "can do" statement and the correct sentence.

_____ 1. I can tell about my current activities.

_____ 2. I can tell about other people's activities.

_____ 3. I can ask about current activities.

_____ 4. I can ask a person's location.

_____ 5. I can tell about a person's location.

_____ 6. I can describe the weather.

a. What are you doing?

b. My friends are watching TV.

c. It's a beautiful day!

d. She's in the living room.

e. I'm studying English.

f. Where are you?

Choose the correct answer.

1. What ____ you doing?
   - Ⓐ is
   - Ⓑ are
   - Ⓒ and
   - Ⓓ our

2. ____ Mr. Clark doing?
   - Ⓐ Where's
   - Ⓑ What
   - Ⓒ What's
   - Ⓓ What are

3. I'm washing my ____.
   - Ⓐ TV
   - Ⓑ yard
   - Ⓒ teeth
   - Ⓓ windows

4. We're doing our ____.
   - Ⓐ radio
   - Ⓑ homework
   - Ⓒ laundromat
   - Ⓓ park

5. They're ____ their kitchen.
   - Ⓐ painting
   - Ⓑ feeding
   - Ⓒ brushing
   - Ⓓ reading

6. She's feeding her ____.
   - Ⓐ car
   - Ⓑ kitchen
   - Ⓒ cat
   - Ⓓ teeth

7. We're ____ our apartment.
   - Ⓐ singing
   - Ⓑ doing
   - Ⓒ brushing
   - Ⓓ cleaning

8. He's painting the ____.
   - Ⓐ breakfast
   - Ⓑ TV
   - Ⓒ wall
   - Ⓓ dog

9. We're ____ our exercises.
   - Ⓐ doing
   - Ⓑ fixing
   - Ⓒ listening to
   - Ⓓ cleaning

10. I'm ____ my e-mail.
   - Ⓐ painting
   - Ⓑ reading
   - Ⓒ watching
   - Ⓓ washing

SKILLS CHECK

Match the "can do" statement and the correct sentence.

____ 1. I can ask about current activities.
____ 2. I can tell about a person's location.
____ 3. I can tell about my daily activities.
____ 4. I can greet someone on the phone.
____ 5. I can tell about other people's activities.
____ 6. I can ask a person's location.

a. Hi!
b. They're washing their clothes.
c. Where's Jenny Chang?
d. He's in the park.
e. What are you doing?
f. I'm brushing my teeth.

Choose the correct answer.

1. Is Helen young _____ old?
- Ⓐ and
- Ⓑ on
- Ⓒ or
- Ⓓ in

2. _____ the food expensive?
- Ⓐ Are
- Ⓑ Is
- Ⓒ It's
- Ⓓ Am

3. A. _____ the weather?
   B. It's sunny.
- Ⓐ What
- Ⓑ How
- Ⓒ Where's
- Ⓓ How's

4. A. Are you married?
   B. Yes, _____.
- Ⓐ I am
- Ⓑ I'm not
- Ⓒ they are
- Ⓓ we aren't

5. A. Is the question easy?
   B. No, _____.
- Ⓐ he isn't
- Ⓑ it is
- Ⓒ it isn't
- Ⓓ they aren't

6. Our car is _____.
- Ⓐ married
- Ⓑ thin
- Ⓒ single
- Ⓓ old

7. The homework is _____.
- Ⓐ handsome
- Ⓑ difficult
- Ⓒ cheap
- Ⓓ rich

8. A. Tell me about your neighbors.
   B. They're _____.
- Ⓐ expensive
- Ⓑ easy
- Ⓒ cloudy
- Ⓓ noisy

9. Our new apartment is _____.
- Ⓐ beautiful
- Ⓑ poor
- Ⓒ married
- Ⓓ heavy

10. A. Are you having a good time?
   B. No. I'm having a _____ time.
- Ⓐ loud
- Ⓑ tall
- Ⓒ terrible
- Ⓓ cold

SKILLS CHECK

Match the "can do" statement and the correct sentence.

_____ **1.** I can describe people.

_____ **2.** I can describe objects.

_____ **3.** I can ask for information.

_____ **4.** I can describe the weather.

_____ **5.** I can call someone on the telephone.

_____ **6.** I can ask about the weather.

a. Tell me about your new boss.

b. Hello. Is this Jim?

c. How's the weather in Miami?

d. They're tall.

e. It's cloudy.

f. Her car is new.

Choose the correct answer.

1. A. Who is he?
   B. He's _____.
   - (A) my daughter
   - (B) in front of our house
   - (C) my grandfather
   - (D) at school

2. A. Where is she?
   B. She's _____.
   - (A) my sister
   - (B) in our apartment
   - (C) vacuuming the rug
   - (D) my husband

3. A. What are they doing?
   B. They're _____.
   - (A) my parents
   - (B) in the living room
   - (C) my niece
   - (D) having dinner

4. He's sleeping _____ the sofa.
   - (A) on
   - (B) in
   - (C) at
   - (D) of

5. My neighbor _____.
   - (A) are making noise
   - (B) is doing
   - (C) is playing the guitar
   - (D) washing her car

6. Our daughter is swimming _____.
   - (A) in the kitchen
   - (B) at the beach
   - (C) in our living room
   - (D) in her bedroom

7. My son is _____ in the park.
   - (A) baking
   - (B) sleeping on a sofa
   - (C) riding his bicycle
   - (D) sitting on his bed

8. We're washing our car _____.
   - (A) in our kitchen
   - (B) on a bench
   - (C) in Apartment 4
   - (D) in front of our apartment building

9. My family and friends are _____ at my wedding.
   - (A) singing and dancing
   - (B) barking
   - (C) skateboarding
   - (D) feeding the birds

10. He's making a lot of noise. He's _____.
    - (A) planting flowers
    - (B) sitting on a bench
    - (C) listening to loud music
    - (D) reading a book

SKILLS CHECK ✓

Match the "can do" statement and the correct sentence.

_____ 1. I can identify my family members.

_____ 2. I can tell about my activities.

_____ 3. I can tell about other people's activities.

_____ 4. I can ask a person's location.

_____ 5. I can tell about a person's location.

_____ 6. I can introduce people.

_____ 7. I can describe a person's emotions.

_____ 8. I can greet people.

a. He's in the park.

b. They're planting flowers.

c. Nice to meet you.

d. I'd like to introduce my sister.

e. She's my daughter.

f. Where is he?

g. I'm baking a cake.

h. He's very angry.

Choose the correct answer.

1. _____ a supermarket around the corner.
   - (A) Is there
   - (B) There
   - (C) Where's
   - (D) There's

2. _____ any children in the building?
   - (A) There
   - (B) Are there
   - (C) There are
   - (D) There's

3. _____ stores are there in the mall?
   - (A) How
   - (B) Are there
   - (C) How many
   - (D) Where are

4. The supermarket is _____ the bank and the gas station.
   - (A) across
   - (B) next
   - (C) between
   - (D) around the corner

5. A. Is there a clinic nearby?
   B. No, _____.
   - (A) there are
   - (B) there isn't
   - (C) it isn't
   - (D) there is

6. There's a laundromat in my _____.
   - (A) closet
   - (B) neighborhood
   - (C) apartment
   - (D) bathroom

7. There are four _____ in my apartment.
   - (A) streets
   - (B) sidewalks
   - (C) buildings
   - (D) rooms

8. The _____ is fixing the stove.
   - (A) superintendent
   - (B) supermarket
   - (C) refrigerator
   - (D) kitchen

9. There's _____ in the bedroom.
   - (A) a window
   - (B) a stove
   - (C) an apartment
   - (D) a mailbox

10. Our neighborhood is in a convenient location. There's _____ near the building.
   - (A) an air conditioner
   - (B) a bus stop
   - (C) an elevator
   - (D) a satellite dish

SKILLS CHECK

Match the "can do" statement and the correct sentence.

_____ 1. I can ask the location of places.

_____ 2. I can give the location of places.

_____ 3. I can express gratitude.

_____ 4. I can describe my home.

_____ 5. I can ask about an apartment for rent.

_____ 6. I can describe my neighborhood.

a. The clinic is next to the bank.

b. It's a very busy and noisy place to live.

c. Is there a refrigerator in the kitchen?

d. Where's the post office?

e. There are two bedrooms in my apartment.

f. Thank you.

Choose the correct answer.

1. _____ are very popular this year.
   Ⓐ Orange blouse
   Ⓑ Shoes yellow
   Ⓒ Striped socks
   Ⓓ Pink dress

2. I'm looking for a pair of _____.
   Ⓐ earring
   Ⓑ pajamas
   Ⓒ purse
   Ⓓ sock

3. _____ your mittens?
   Ⓐ Those
   Ⓑ Are there
   Ⓒ Is this
   Ⓓ Are these

4. Excuse me. I think _____ my glove.
   Ⓐ that's
   Ⓑ this
   Ⓒ there's
   Ⓓ is that

5. _____ briefcase _____ very nice.
   Ⓐ Those . . . are
   Ⓑ That's . . . is
   Ⓒ This . . . is
   Ⓓ This is . . . that's

6. My favorite color is _____.
   Ⓐ large
   Ⓑ striped
   Ⓒ clean
   Ⓓ purple

7. It's cold today. Where are my _____?
   Ⓐ mittens
   Ⓑ glasses
   Ⓒ earrings
   Ⓓ watches

8. It's raining. Where's my _____?
   Ⓐ briefcase
   Ⓑ umbrella
   Ⓒ necklace
   Ⓓ bracelet

9. It's snowing. Where are my _____?
   Ⓐ pajamas
   Ⓑ belts
   Ⓒ boots
   Ⓓ earrings

10. My brother is wearing a blue suit, a red tie, and a white _____.
    Ⓐ dress
    Ⓑ shirt
    Ⓒ skirt
    Ⓓ briefcase

SKILLS CHECK

Match the "can do" statement and the correct sentence.

_____ 1. I can ask for help in a store.

_____ 2. I can offer to help a customer.

_____ 3. I can describe clothing.

_____ 4. I can express gratitude.

_____ 5. I can agree with someone.

_____ 6. I can disagree with someone.

_____ 7. I can compliment someone.

_____ 8. I can apologize.

a. Thanks.

b. I don't think so.

c. Excuse me. I'm looking for a dress.

d. You're right.

e. That's a very nice hat.

f. These boots are blue.

g. I'm sorry.

h. May I help you?

Choose the correct answer.

1. Where _____ ?
   - Ⓐ you live
   - Ⓑ you do live
   - Ⓒ do you live
   - Ⓓ live you

2. What language _____ ?
   - Ⓐ he speaks
   - Ⓑ do he speak
   - Ⓒ he does speak
   - Ⓓ does he speak

3. We're Carol and Dan. _____ in London.
   - Ⓐ We work
   - Ⓑ They work
   - Ⓒ We works
   - Ⓓ Do we work

4. Carla _____ the newspaper every day.
   - Ⓐ read
   - Ⓑ does she read
   - Ⓒ she read
   - Ⓓ reads

5. What _____ every day?
   - Ⓐ you do
   - Ⓑ do you do
   - Ⓒ do you
   - Ⓓ does you do

6. I'm from Canada. I speak _____ .
   - Ⓐ Canadian
   - Ⓑ Toronto
   - Ⓒ English and French
   - Ⓓ language

7. We eat Mexican _____ every day.
   - Ⓐ music
   - Ⓑ food
   - Ⓒ shopping malls
   - Ⓓ songs

8. I _____ my grandparents every weekend.
   - Ⓐ visit
   - Ⓑ listen
   - Ⓒ paint
   - Ⓓ speak

9. My sister _____ a bus.
   - Ⓐ works
   - Ⓑ talks
   - Ⓒ calls
   - Ⓓ drives

10. My husband _____ cars.
    - Ⓐ plays
    - Ⓑ sells
    - Ⓒ lives
    - Ⓓ reads

SKILLS CHECK

Match the "can do" statement and the correct sentence.

_____ 1. I can ask a person's name.

_____ 2. I can tell where I live.

_____ 3. I can tell what language I speak.

_____ 4. I can tell about my nationality.

_____ 5. I can tell about my work.

_____ 6. I can ask about a person's work.

_____ 7. I can describe a person's emotions.

_____ 8. I can hesitate while I'm thinking.

a. I'm Greek.

b. What does she do?

c. Hmm. Well, . . .

d. I live in Seoul.

e. He's sad.

f. What's your name?

g. I drive a taxi.

h. I speak Spanish.

Choose the correct answer.

1. _____ Michael _____ Italian food?
   Ⓐ Does . . . likes
   Ⓑ Do . . . like
   Ⓒ Does . . . like
   Ⓓ Do . . . likes

2. _____ your parents _____ English?
   Ⓐ Does . . . speak
   Ⓑ Do . . . speaks
   Ⓒ Are . . . speak
   Ⓓ Do . . . speak

3. A. Does your sister play tennis?
   B. Yes, _____.
   Ⓐ she doesn't
   Ⓑ she does
   Ⓒ she do
   Ⓓ does she

4. A. Do your friends sing in the choir?
   B. No, _____.
   Ⓐ do they
   Ⓑ don't they
   Ⓒ they don't
   Ⓓ they do

5. Bob _____ work on Saturday. He _____ on Sunday.
   Ⓐ doesn't . . . works
   Ⓑ does . . . work
   Ⓒ don't . . . work
   Ⓓ does . . . works

6. I ride _____ every day.
   Ⓐ American food
   Ⓑ a different kind of sport
   Ⓒ books
   Ⓓ my bicycle

7. My daughter plays _____.
   Ⓐ a musical instrument
   Ⓑ karate
   Ⓒ dinner
   Ⓓ novels

8. I work during the week. I don't work on the weekend. I don't work on _____.
   Ⓐ Tuesday
   Ⓑ Sunday
   Ⓒ Thursday
   Ⓓ Monday

9. I read every day. I usually read _____.
   Ⓐ videos
   Ⓑ game shows
   Ⓒ classical music
   Ⓓ short stories

10. Janet is very athletic. She _____ every weekend.
    Ⓐ sings
    Ⓑ plays in the orchestra
    Ⓒ plays tennis
    Ⓓ sees a play

SKILLS CHECK

Match the "can do" statement and the correct sentence.

_____ 1. I can say the days of the week.

_____ 2. I can talk about work activities.

_____ 3. I can talk about likes.

_____ 4. I can talk about dislikes.

_____ 5. I can describe recreational activities.

_____ 6. I can describe people.

_____ 7. I can start a conversation.

_____ 8. I can ask questions to make small talk.

a. I like Chinese food.

b. On Sunday I ride my bike.

c. Sheldon is a very shy person.

d. Mr. Garcia works at the post office.

e. Tell me, . . .

f. What kind of movies do you like?

g. Sunday, Monday, Tuesday, . . .

h. I don't like American food.

Choose the correct answer.

1. I _____ long hair and my brother _____ short hair.
   - Ⓐ has . . . has
   - Ⓑ have . . . has
   - Ⓒ have . . . have
   - Ⓓ has . . . have

2. A. How often do you see your neighbor?
   B. I see _____ every day.
   - Ⓐ them
   - Ⓑ us
   - Ⓒ her
   - Ⓓ me

3. A. How often do your cousins visit you?
   B. They visit _____ every summer.
   - Ⓐ them
   - Ⓑ him
   - Ⓒ her
   - Ⓓ us

4. I often _____ TV. My wife rarely _____ it.
   - Ⓐ watch . . . watch
   - Ⓑ watches . . . watches
   - Ⓒ watch . . . watches
   - Ⓓ watches . . . watch

5. Mr. DeLuca is _____ landlord. I like _____ very much.
   - Ⓐ my . . . him
   - Ⓑ our . . . her
   - Ⓒ your . . . them
   - Ⓓ my . . . us

6. Marie _____ her computer every day.
   - Ⓐ writes
   - Ⓑ reads
   - Ⓒ uses
   - Ⓓ makes

7. I usually take the bus to work. I _____.
   - Ⓐ always drive
   - Ⓑ usually drive
   - Ⓒ drive every day
   - Ⓓ rarely drive

8. I wash my car every Sunday. I wash it _____.
   - Ⓐ once a day
   - Ⓑ once a week
   - Ⓒ once a month
   - Ⓓ once a year

9. My son has _____ eyes.
   - Ⓐ curly
   - Ⓑ blue
   - Ⓒ blond
   - Ⓓ tall

10. We never go out on the weekend. We always _____.
   - Ⓐ go to the movies
   - Ⓑ go to parties
   - Ⓒ go dancing
   - Ⓓ watch videos at home

SKILLS CHECK

Match the "can do" statement and the correct sentence.

_____ **1.** I can talk about everyday activities.

_____ **2.** I can tell about family members.

_____ **3.** I can describe people.

_____ **4.** I can give my occupation.

_____ **5.** I can give my marital status.

_____ **6.** I can compare myself with another person.

_____ **7.** I can ask for information.

_____ **8.** I can react to information.

a. I'm a journalist.

b. Linda usually eats in the cafeteria.

c. Oh, really? That's interesting.

d. I'm single.

e. We're very different.

f. He has long, straight hair.

g. Tell me about your sister.

h. Our grandchildren call us every Sunday.

Choose the correct answer.

1. _____ a big breakfast today because she's very hungry.
   - Ⓐ She has
   - Ⓑ She's having
   - Ⓒ She doesn't have
   - Ⓓ She isn't having

2. _____ because I'm angry. I always _____ when I'm angry.
   - Ⓐ I shout . . . shouting
   - Ⓑ I'm shouting . . . shouting
   - Ⓒ I'm shouting . . . shout
   - Ⓓ I shouting . . . shout

3. I never _____ to work, but _____ to work today.
   - Ⓐ walk . . . I walk
   - Ⓑ walking . . . I'm walking
   - Ⓒ walking . . . I walk
   - Ⓓ walk . . . I'm walking

4. Why _____ today? He hardly ever _____.
   - Ⓐ is he smiling . . . smiles
   - Ⓑ he smiles . . . smiles
   - Ⓒ does he smile . . . is smiling
   - Ⓓ does he smile . . . smiles

5. It's raining. People who usually _____ their bicycles _____ them today.
   - Ⓐ ride . . . are riding
   - Ⓑ riding . . . ride
   - Ⓒ ride . . . aren't riding
   - Ⓓ don't ride . . . don't ride

6. I usually go to the doctor when I'm _____.
   - Ⓐ happy
   - Ⓑ hungry
   - Ⓒ sick
   - Ⓓ angry

7. I'm _____ because I'm tired.
   - Ⓐ biting my nails
   - Ⓑ yawning
   - Ⓒ smiling
   - Ⓓ perspiring

8. She's walking to school today because her _____ is broken.
   - Ⓐ computer
   - Ⓑ sink
   - Ⓒ lamp
   - Ⓓ bicycle

9. The receptionist at our office _____ the telephone.
   - Ⓐ types
   - Ⓑ answers
   - Ⓒ rushes
   - Ⓓ takes

10. I'm a police officer. Every morning I _____ on Main Street.
    - Ⓐ deliver
    - Ⓑ walk
    - Ⓒ direct traffic
    - Ⓓ make

SKILLS CHECK

Match the "can do" statement and the correct sentence.

_____ 1. I can describe my feelings and emotions.

_____ 2. I can describe how I react to things.

_____ 3. I can ask about a person's activity.

_____ 4. I can express surprise.

_____ 5. I can describe a repair problem.

_____ 6. I can react to bad news.

_____ 7. I can describe people's work.

a. My sink is broken.

b. What are you doing?

c. Mail carriers deliver mail.

d. I'm happy.

e. I'm sorry to hear that.

f. That's strange!

g. When I'm nervous, I perspire.

Choose the correct answer.

1. I _____, but I _____.
   Ⓐ can't ski . . . can't skate
   Ⓑ can ski . . . can't skate
   Ⓒ can ski . . . can skate
   Ⓓ can't ski . . . can ski

2. Carlos is busy today. He _____ fix his car.
   Ⓐ has to
   Ⓑ has
   Ⓒ have
   Ⓓ have to

3. Please fill out this form in duplicate.
   You _____ use a pencil. You _____ use a pen.
   Ⓐ can . . . have to
   Ⓑ have to . . . have to
   Ⓒ can't . . . have to
   Ⓓ have to . . . can

4. Roberta is a very bad singer. She _____ sing very well.
   Ⓐ can
   Ⓑ has to
   Ⓒ can't
   Ⓓ doesn't have to

5. A. Can Timothy repair cars?
   B. No, he _____, but he _____ repair bicycles.
   Ⓐ can . . . can't
   Ⓑ can't . . . can't
   Ⓒ has to . . . can
   Ⓓ can't . . . can

6. Ramon can _____. He's looking for a job as a secretary.
   Ⓐ bake
   Ⓑ paint
   Ⓒ type
   Ⓓ ski

7. Ann can _____. She's looking for a job as a mechanic.
   Ⓐ repair cars
   Ⓑ fix stoves
   Ⓒ skate
   Ⓓ paint pictures

8. Ivan can _____. He's looking for a job as a salesperson.
   Ⓐ file
   Ⓑ operate equipment
   Ⓒ use tools
   Ⓓ take inventory

9. I'm a construction worker. I can _____.
   Ⓐ use business software
   Ⓑ build things
   Ⓒ take inventory
   Ⓓ use a cash register

10. I'm sick. I can't go to work today.
    I have to _____.
    Ⓐ visit my friends
    Ⓑ do my exercises
    Ⓒ go to the doctor
    Ⓓ wash my car

SKILLS CHECK

Match the "can do" statement and the correct sentence.

_____ 1. I can tell my occupation.

_____ 2. I can ask about a person's skills.

_____ 3. I can tell about my skills.

_____ 4. I can express my job interests.

_____ 5. I can express inability to do something.

_____ 6. I can express obligation.

_____ 7. I can describe a person's emotions.

_____ 8. I can apologize.

a. I can drive a truck.

b. I'm looking for a job as a baker.

c. He's annoyed.

d. I'm a mechanic.

e. I have to do my homework.

f. I'm sorry.

g. Can you use a cash register?

h. I can't go to a movie.

Choose the correct answer.

1. I'm looking forward to this weekend.
   We're _____ a concert.
   ⓐ going
   ⓑ going to go
   ⓒ going to go to
   ⓓ go to

2. A. What's the forecast?
   B. According to the newspaper, _____
      tomorrow.
   ⓐ it rains
   ⓑ it's going be sunny
   ⓒ it's be foggy
   ⓓ it's going to rain

3. _____ the train leave?
   ⓐ When
   ⓑ What time
   ⓒ What time does
   ⓓ When is the time when

4. The bus leaves _____.
   ⓐ ten forty-five
   ⓑ at nine fifteen
   ⓒ noon
   ⓓ in a quarter to five

5. I _____ see a movie, but my friend
   _____ go to the park.
   ⓐ want . . . want
   ⓑ want . . . wants
   ⓒ want to . . . want to
   ⓓ want to . . . wants to

6. June is my favorite _____.
   ⓐ week of the year
   ⓑ day of the week
   ⓒ month of the year
   ⓓ holiday

7. We're going to the beach tomorrow.
   It's going to _____.
   ⓐ rain
   ⓑ snow
   ⓒ be cold and cloudy
   ⓓ be warm and sunny

8. My sister and I are going to a baseball
   game at two o'clock _____.
   ⓐ tomorrow afternoon
   ⓑ this morning
   ⓒ this evening
   ⓓ tonight

9. I'm going to save a lot of money because
   I want to _____.
   ⓐ go to the library
   ⓑ see a movie
   ⓒ buy a car
   ⓓ have a picnic

10. We're having breakfast now.
    We're going to have lunch _____.
    ⓐ at noon
    ⓑ at midnight
    ⓒ tonight
    ⓓ tomorrow morning

SKILLS CHECK ✓

Match the "can do" statement and the correct sentence.

_____ 1. I can give the time.
_____ 2. I can say the months of the year.
_____ 3. I can name the seasons.
_____ 4. I can ask about future plans.
_____ 5. I can tell about future plans.
_____ 6. I can ask about the weather.
_____ 7. I can ask the time.
_____ 8. I can tell about future weather.

a. Spring, summer, winter, fall.
b. What are you going to do tomorrow?
c. It's going to be sunny.
d. I'm going to go swimming.
e. What time is it?
f. It's two o'clock.
g. What's the forecast?
h. January, February, March, . . .

Choose the correct answer.

1. ____ all morning today, and now I have a headache.
   Ⓐ I study
   Ⓑ I studied
   Ⓒ I'm going to study
   Ⓓ I'm studying

2. David ____ TV today. ____ every day.
   Ⓐ watches . . . He watches
   Ⓑ watch . . . He's going to watch
   Ⓒ watched . . . He watches
   Ⓓ watched . . . He's watching

3. ____ yesterday, and ____ tomorrow.
   Ⓐ I'm going to clean . . . I cleaned
   Ⓑ I cleaned . . . I'm going to clean
   Ⓒ I clean . . . I'm going to clean
   Ⓓ I'm cleaning . . . I'm cleaning

4. I ____ for the bus all morning.
   Ⓐ waited
   Ⓑ rode
   Ⓒ finished
   Ⓓ wanted

5. I ____ all afternoon, and now I have a terrible backache.
   Ⓐ sang
   Ⓑ talked
   Ⓒ rested
   Ⓓ sat

6. Amanda ____ her broken front steps.
   Ⓐ worked
   Ⓑ fixed
   Ⓒ served
   Ⓓ asked

7. Henry ate cookies all day, and now he has ____.
   Ⓐ a fever
   Ⓑ an earache
   Ⓒ a cold
   Ⓓ a stomachache

8. I ____ at work at 9:00 this morning.
   Ⓐ arrived
   Ⓑ showed
   Ⓒ rode
   Ⓓ turned

9. My son ____ his homework at 8:30.
   Ⓐ looked
   Ⓑ stayed
   Ⓒ finished
   Ⓓ watched

10. We ____ a video of our trip to Japan.
    Ⓐ asked
    Ⓑ showed
    Ⓒ sang
    Ⓓ rested

SKILLS CHECK

Match the "can do" statement and the correct sentence.

____ 1. I can describe ailments.

____ 2. I can ask about a person's health.

____ 3. I can express sympathy.

____ 4. I can say that I feel well.

____ 5. I can say that I don't feel well.

____ 6. I can ask about past activities.

____ 7. I can tell about past activities.

____ 8. I can call someone.

a. I'm sorry to hear that.

b. I feel terrible.

c. Hello. This is Bob Wilson.

d. What did you do yesterday?

e. How do you feel today?

f. I worked all day yesterday.

g. I feel fine.

h. I have a headache.

Choose the correct answer.

1. _____ the news this morning?
   - Ⓐ You listen to
   - Ⓑ Did you listened to
   - Ⓒ Did you listen to
   - Ⓓ Listened you to

2. _____ yesterday evening?
   - Ⓐ What you did
   - Ⓑ What did you do
   - Ⓒ What did you did
   - Ⓓ What did you

3. A. Did you see your friends yesterday?
   B. _____
   - Ⓐ Yes, they did.
   - Ⓑ Yes, did I.
   - Ⓒ Yes, I did.
   - Ⓓ No, I did.

4. A. Did Maria take the bus today?
   B. No, _____. She _____ the train.
   - Ⓐ she didn't . . . took
   - Ⓑ she did . . . took
   - Ⓒ didn't she . . . didn't take
   - Ⓓ she didn't . . . didn't take

5. I _____ to the park. I _____ to the bank.
   - Ⓐ didn't went . . . went
   - Ⓑ not went . . . did go
   - Ⓒ went not . . . did went
   - Ⓓ didn't go . . . went

6. Susan arrived late for work because she missed the _____.
   - Ⓐ apartment
   - Ⓑ office
   - Ⓒ bus
   - Ⓓ newspaper

7. I met a _____ on the way to work today.
   - Ⓐ book
   - Ⓑ friend
   - Ⓒ bank
   - Ⓓ car

8. After he _____ the train, Omar walked to the office.
   - Ⓐ got off
   - Ⓑ got up
   - Ⓒ had
   - Ⓓ went

9. I _____ my house at 7:45 to go to school.
   - Ⓐ arrived
   - Ⓑ took
   - Ⓒ saw
   - Ⓓ left

10. After work today, I _____ some groceries.
    - Ⓐ ate
    - Ⓑ had
    - Ⓒ bought
    - Ⓓ made

SKILLS CHECK ✓

Match the "can do" statement and the correct sentence.

_____ 1. I can ask about past activities.

_____ 2. I can tell about past activities.

_____ 3. I can apologize for something.

_____ 4. I can tell about obligation.

_____ 5. I can give an excuse for lateness.

_____ 6. I can describe ailments.

a. I had to go to the dentist.

b. I'm sorry I'm late.

c. We went to the supermarket.

d. I had a stomachache.

e. What did you do yesterday?

f. I missed the bus.

Choose the correct answer.

1. She ___ upset, and her parents ___ upset, too.
   - (A) was . . . was
   - (B) were . . . was
   - (C) was . . . were
   - (D) were . . . were

2. Before we bought an air conditioner, our apartment ___ always hot. Now our apartment ___ very comfortable.
   - (A) is . . . is
   - (B) is . . . was
   - (C) was . . . is
   - (D) was . . . was

3. Carlos ___ at work yesterday. He stayed home because he ___ sick.
   - (A) was . . . was
   - (B) wasn't . . . was
   - (C) wasn't . . . wasn't
   - (D) was . . . wasn't

4. My wife and I ___ late for the plane. We ___ early.
   - (A) wasn't . . . was
   - (B) weren't . . . were
   - (C) were . . . were
   - (D) weren't . . . weren't

5. I ___ sleep well because I ___ tired.
   - (A) wasn't . . . wasn't
   - (B) didn't . . . weren't
   - (C) didn't . . . was
   - (D) didn't . . . wasn't

6. I ate a big breakfast today because I was very ___.
   - (A) dull
   - (B) full
   - (C) hungry
   - (D) shiny

7. We didn't like the restaurant because the food ___.
   - (A) was bad
   - (B) was sad
   - (C) wasn't bad
   - (D) was quiet

8. My best friend moved to South America. I really ___ her.
   - (A) look forward to
   - (B) meet
   - (C) miss
   - (D) see

9. I usually ___ with my friends over the Internet.
   - (A) grow up
   - (B) go
   - (C) see
   - (D) communicate

10. We cleaned our living room windows because ___.
   - (A) they were enormous
   - (B) they were dirty
   - (C) they weren't dirty
   - (D) they were clean

SKILLS CHECK

Match the "can do" statement and the correct sentence.

____ 1. I can describe my feelings and emotions.

____ 2. I can describe my health.

____ 3. I can describe an object.

____ 4. I can ask for a recommendation.

____ 5. I can give a recommendation.

____ 6. I can ask about past activities.

____ 7. I can ask about the weather.

a. I recommend *Presto* Toothpaste.

b. Can you recommend a good soap?

c. I was sick.

d. Was it cold yesterday?

e. My armchair was uncomfortable.

f. I was sad.

g. Did you go to the doctor yesterday?

Listening Scripts

Chapter 1 – Page 5

Listen and choose the correct answer.

1. A. What's your name?
   B. Mary Black.
2. A. What's your address?
   B. Two sixty-five Main Street.
3. A. What's your apartment number?
   B. Five C.
4. A. What's your telephone number?
   B. Two five nine – four oh eight seven.
5. A. What's your social security number?
   B. Oh three two – eight nine – six one seven nine.
6. A. What's your e-mail address?
   B. maryb-at-worldnet-dot-com.

Chapter 2 – Page 15

WHAT'S THE WORD?

Listen and choose the correct answer.

1. Mr. and Mrs. Lee are in the park.
2. Jim is in the hospital.
3. She's in the living room.
4. He's in the kitchen.
5. They're in the basement.
6. We're in the yard.

WHERE ARE THEY?

Listen and choose the correct place.

1. A. Where's David?
   B. He's in the living room.
2. A. Where's Patty?
   B. She's in the bedroom.
3. A. Where are Mr. and Mrs. Kim?
   B. They're in the yard.
4. A. Where are you?
   B. I'm in the bathroom.
5. A. Where's the telephone book?
   B. It's in the kitchen.
6. A. Where are you and John?
   B. We're in the basement.

Chapter 3 – Page 23

Listen and choose the correct answer.

1. What are you doing?
2. What's Mr. Carter doing?
3. What's Ms. Miller doing?
4. What are Jim and Jane doing?
5. What are you and Peter doing?
6. What am I doing?

Side by Side Gazette – Page 26

Listen to the messages on Bob's machine. Match the messages.

You have seven messages.

Message Number One: "Hello. I'm calling for Robert White. This is Henry Drake. Mr. White, please call me at 427-9168. That's 427-9168. Thank you." [*beep*]

Message Number Two: "Hi, Bob! It's Patty. How are you? Call me!" [*beep*]

Message Number Three: "Bob? Hi. This is Kevin Carter from your guitar class. My phone number is 298-4577." [*beep*]

Message Number Four: "Mr. White? This is Linda Lee, from the social security office. Please call me. My telephone number is 969-0159." [*beep*]

Message Number Five: "Hello, Bob? This is Jim. I'm in the park. We're playing baseball. Call me, okay? My cell phone number is 682-4630." [*beep*]

Message Number Six: "Hello. Mr. White? This is Mrs. Lane on River Street. Your dog is in my yard. Call me at 731-0248." [*beep*]

Message Number Seven: "Hello, Bob. This is Dad. I'm at home. I'm reading the newspaper. Mom is planting flowers in the yard. It's a beautiful day. Where are you? What are you doing? Call us." [*beep*]

Chapter 4 – Page 33

Listen and choose the correct answer.

1. What are you eating?
2. What is she reading?
3. What is he playing?
4. What are they painting?
5. What are you watching?
6. What is he washing?

Chapter 5 – Page 43

WHAT'S THE ANSWER?

Listen and choose the correct answer.

1. Tell me about your apartment.
2. Tell me about your new car.
3. Tell me about your neighbors.
4. How's the weather?
5. Tell me about your hotel.
6. How's the food at the restaurant?

TRUE OR FALSE?

Listen to the conversation. Then answer True or False.

A. Hello.
B. Hello. Is this Betty?
A. Yes, it is.
B. Hi, Betty. This is Louise. I'm calling from Mud Beach.
A. From Mud Beach?
B. Yes. I'm on vacation in Mud Beach for a few days.
A. How's the weather in Mud Beach?
B. It's terrible! It's cold, and it's cloudy.
A. Cold and cloudy? What a shame! How's the hotel?
B. The hotel is terrible! It's old, it's noisy, and the rooms are very small.
A. I'm sorry to hear that. Tell me about the restaurants.
B. The restaurants in Mud Beach are expensive, and the food isn't very good. In fact, I'm having problems with my stomach.
A. What a shame! So, Louise, what are you doing?
B. I'm sitting in my room, and I'm watching TV. I'm not having a very good time.
A. I'm sorry to hear that.

Chapter 6 – Page 51

QUIET OR NOISY?

Listen to the sentence. Are the people quiet or noisy?

1. He's listening to loud music.
2. She's reading.
3. He's sleeping.
4. The band is playing.
5. Everybody is singing and dancing.
6. He's studying.

WHAT DO YOU HEAR?

Listen to the sound. What do you hear? Choose the correct answer.

1. [Sound: singing]
2. [Sound: crying]

3. [Sound: vacuuming]
4. [Sound: laughing]
5. [Sound: drums]

Side by Side Gazette – Page 54

Listen to the weather reports. Match the weather and the cities.

This is Robby T. with the weather report from WXBC. It's a hot day in Honolulu today. The temperature here is one hundred degrees, and everybody is swimming at the beach.

This is Annie Lu with the weather report from WCLD in Atlanta. It's snowing here in Atlanta today, and everybody is at home.

This is Herbie Ross with today's weather from KFTG radio. It's warm and sunny here in Los Angeles today. The temperature is seventy degrees. It's a beautiful day.

This is Jimmy G. with your weather on CHME radio. It's cool and sunny here in Toronto today. It's a very nice day.

This is Lisa Lee with your WQRZ weather report. It's cold and cloudy in Chicago today. The temperature here is thirty-two degrees. Yes, it's a cold and cloudy day!

Chapter 7 – Page 65

WHAT PLACES DO YOU HEAR?

Listen and choose the correct places.

Ex.: My neighborhood is very nice. There's a supermarket across the street, and there's a video store around the corner.

1. My neighborhood is very convenient. There's a bank around the corner and a laundromat across the street.
2. My neighborhood is very noisy. There's a fire station next to my building, and there's a gas station across the street.
3. The sidewalks in my neighborhood are very busy. There's a school across the street and a department store around the corner.
4. There are many small stores in the center of my town. There's a bakery, a drug store, and a book store.
5. My neighborhood is very busy. There's a hotel across the street, and the hotel is between a hospital and a health club.

TRUE OR FALSE?

Listen to the conversation. Then answer True or False.

A. Tell me about the apartment.
B. There's a large living room, a large kitchen, a nice bathroom, and a very nice bedroom.
A. How many closets are there in the apartment?
B. There's a closet in the bedroom and a closet in the living room.
A. Oh, I see. And how many windows are there in the living room?
B. There are four windows in the living room.
A. Four windows?
B. Yes. That's right.
A. Tell me. Is there a superintendent in the building?
B. Yes, there is.
A. And are there washing machines in the basement?
B. Yes, there are. There are three washing machines.
A. Oh, good. Tell me, is there an elevator in the building?
B. No, there isn't. But there's a fire escape.

Chapter 8 – Page 75

WHAT'S THE WORD?

Listen and choose the correct answer.

1. A. May I help you?
   B. Yes, please. I'm looking for a blouse.
2. A. Can I help you?
   B. Yes, please. I'm looking for a pair of boots.
3. A. May I help you?
   B. Yes, please. I'm looking for a necklace.
4. A. Can I help you?
   B. Yes, please. I'm looking for a raincoat.
5. A. May I help you?
   B. Yes, please. I'm looking for a pair of stockings.
6. A. Can I help you?
   B. Yes, please. I'm looking for a shirt.

WHICH WORD DO YOU HEAR?

Listen and choose the correct answer.

1. These jackets are expensive.
2. I'm looking for a leather belt.
3. I'm wearing my new wool sweater.
4. Suits are over there.
5. Is this your shoe?
6. Polka dot ties are very popular this year.

Side by Side Gazette – Page 77

Listen to these announcements in a clothing store. Match the clothing and the aisles.

Attention, J-Mart Shoppers! Are you looking for a black leather jacket? Black leather jackets are very popular this year! There are a lot of black leather jackets at J-Mart today! They're in Aisle 9, next to the coats.

Attention, J-Mart Shoppers! Are you looking for a pair of vinyl gloves? Vinyl gloves are very popular this year! Well, there are a lot of vinyl gloves at J-Mart today! They're in Aisle 5, across from the hats.

Attention, J-Mart Shoppers! Are you looking for a blouse? Is red your favorite color? Red blouses are very popular this year! There are a lot of red blouses at J-Mart today. They're in Aisle 7, next to the dresses.

Attention, J-Mart Shoppers! Are you looking for a special gift for your mother, your wife, or your sister? A silver bracelet is a special gift for that special person. All our silver bracelets are in Aisle 1, across from the earrings.

Attention, J-Mart Shoppers! Are you looking for a special gift for your father, your husband, or your brother? A polka dot tie is a special gift for that special person. All our polka dot ties are in Aisle 11, next to the belts.

Chapter 9 – Page 84

Listen and choose the correct answer.

1. My brother lives in Chicago.
2. My name is Peter. I work in an office.
3. This is my friend Carla. She speaks Italian.
4. My sister drives a bus in Chicago.
5. We read the newspaper every day.
6. My parents visit their friends every weekend.
7. Charlie cooks in a Greek restaurant.
8. My brother and I paint houses.
9. My friend Betty calls me every day.
10. My parents usually shop at the mall.

Chapter 10 – Page 93

WHAT'S THE WORD?

Listen and choose the word you hear.

1. Do you work on Monday?
2. Does your daughter go to this school?
3. We do a different activity every Sunday.
4. Larry doesn't play a sport.
5. We don't go to Stanley's Restaurant.
6. Sally goes to a health club every week.
7. She baby-sits for her neighbors every Thursday.
8. They go to work every morning.

Listen and choose the correct response.

1. Do you speak Korean?
2. Does Mrs. Wilson go to Stanley's Restaurant?
3. Does your sister live in Los Angeles?
4. Do you and your brother clean the house together?
5. Does your husband like American food?
6. Do you go to school on the weekend?
7. Do you and your friends play tennis?
8. Does your cousin live in this neighborhood?

Side by Side Gazette – Page 98

You're calling the International Cafe! Listen to the recorded announcement. Match the day of the week and the kind of entertainment.

Hello! This is the International Cafe—your special place for wonderful entertainment every day of the week! Every day the International Cafe presents a different kind of entertainment. On Monday, Antonio Bello plays Italian classical music. On Tuesday, Miguel Garcia reads Spanish poetry. On Wednesday, Amanda Silva sings Brazilian jazz. On Thursday, Nina Markova reads Russian short stories. On Friday, Hiroshi Tanaka plays Japanese rock music. On Saturday, Rita Rivera sings Mexican popular music. And on Sunday, Slim Wilkins sings American country music. So come to the International Cafe—your special place for wonderful entertainment . . . every day of the week!

Chapter 11 – Page 105

Listen to the conversations. Who and what are they talking about?

1. A. How often do you visit him?
   B. I visit him every week.
2. A. How often do you wash them?
   B. I wash them every year.
3. A. Do you write to her very often?
   B. I write to her every month.
4. A. Is it broken?
   B. Yes. I'm fixing it now.
5. A. How often do you see them?
   B. I see them every day.
6. A. How often do you use it?
   B. I use it all the time.
7. A. When does he wash it?
   B. He washes it every Sunday.
8. A. Do you see him very often?
   B. No. I rarely see him.
9. A. Do you study with them very often?
   B. Yes. I study with them all the time.

Chapter 12 – Page 112

Listen and choose the correct answer.

1. What are you doing?
2. What does the office assistant do?
3. What's the receptionist doing?
4. Is he tired?
5. What do you do when you're scared?
6. Where do you usually study?

Side by Side Gazette – Page 115

Listen to these news reports. Match the news and the city.

A. You're listening to WBOS in Boston. And now here's Randy Ryan with today's news.
B. Good morning. Well, the people in Boston who usually take the subway to work aren't taking it today. There's a big problem with the subway system in Boston.

A. You're listening to KSAC in Sacramento. And now here's Jessica Chen with the morning news.

B. Good morning. The big news here in Sacramento is the traffic! Sacramento police officers are on strike today, and nobody is directing traffic. There are traffic problems all around the city!

A. This is WCHI in Chicago. And now here's Mike Maxwell with today's news.
B. Good morning. It's snowing very hard in Chicago right now. As a result, the streets of the city are empty. People aren't walking or driving to work. There aren't any trucks or buses on the street. And mail carriers aren't delivering the mail.

A. You're listening to CTOR in Toronto. And now here's Mark Mitchell with today's news.
B. It's a quiet Tuesday morning in Toronto. There aren't any bad traffic problems right now, and there aren't any problems with the subway system or the buses.

A. You're listening to WMIA in Miami. And now here's today's news.
B. Good morning. This is Rita Rodriguez with the news. The children of Miami who usually take school buses to school aren't taking them this morning. The men and women who drive the school buses are on strike. Some children are walking to school today. Many students are staying home.

Chapter 13 – Page 121

CAN OR CAN'T?

Listen and choose the word you hear.

1. I can speak Spanish.
2. He can't paint.
3. She can type.
4. We can't build things.
5. They can use tools.
6. We can't operate equipment.

WHAT CAN THEY DO?

Listen and choose what each person can do.

1. He can't file. He can type.
2. They can cook. They can't bake.
3. She can repair locks. She can't repair stoves.
4. I can't drive a truck. I can drive a bus.
5. He can teach French. He can't teach English.
6. We can take inventory. We can't paint.

Chapter 14 – Page 132

Listen and choose the words you hear.

1. A. When are you going to buy a computer?
   B. Tomorrow.
2. A. When are your neighbors going to move?
   B. Next November.
3. A. When are you going to visit me?
   B. Next month.
4. A. When are you going to do your laundry?
   B. This evening.
5. A. When are you going to begin your vacation?
   B. This Sunday.
6. A. When are we going to go to the concert?
   B. This Thursday.
7. A. When are you going to wash the windows?
   B. This afternoon.
8. A. When is she going to get her driver's license?
   B. Next week.
9. A. When is your daughter going to finish college?
   B. Next winter.
10. A. When is the landlord going to fix the kitchen sink?
    B. At once.

Side by Side Gazette – Page 140

Listen and match the theaters and the movies.

Thank you for calling the Multiplex Cinema! The Multiplex Cinema has five theaters with the best movies in town!

Now showing in Theater One: *The Spanish Dancer,* a film from Spain about the life of the famous dancer Carlos Montero. Show times are at one fifteen, three thirty, and seven o'clock.

Now showing in Theater Two: *When Are You Going to Call the Plumber?,* starring Julie Richards and Harry Grant. In this comedy, a husband and wife have a lot of problems in their new house. Show times are at two thirty, four forty-five, and seven fifteen.

Now showing in Theater Three: *The Fortune Teller.* In this film from Brazil, a woman tells people all the things that are going to happen in their lives. Show times are at five o'clock, seven forty-five, and ten fifteen.

Now showing in Theater Four: *The Time Zone Machine,* the exciting new science fiction movie. Professor Stanley Carrington's new machine can send people to different time zones around the world. Show times are at five fifteen, eight o'clock, and ten thirty. There's also a special show at midnight.

Now showing in Theater Five: *Tomorrow Is Right Now.* In this new drama, a truck driver from Australia falls in love with a businesswoman from Paris. Where are they going to live, and what are they going to tell their friends? See it and find out! Show times are at six o'clock, eight thirty, and ten forty-five.

The Multiplex Cinema is on Harrison Avenue, across from the shopping mall. So come and see a movie at the Multiplex Cinema. You're going to have a good time! Thank you, and have a nice day!

Chapter 15 – Page 147

Listen and choose the word you hear.

1. We plant flowers in our garden in the spring.
2. I worked at the office all day.
3. They studied English all morning.
4. Mr. and Mrs. Jones sit in their living room all day.
5. They drank lemonade all summer.
6. I waited for the bus all morning.
7. They finish their work at five o'clock.
8. We invited our friends to the party.
9. I eat cheese and crackers.
10. She cleaned her apartment all afternoon.
11. We wash our clothes at the laundromat.
12. He watched TV all evening.

Chapter 16 – Page 155

Listen and put a check next to all the things these people did today.

Carla got up early this morning. She took a shower, she had breakfast, and she took the subway to work. She didn't have lunch today. She left work at five thirty, and she met her mother at six o'clock. They had dinner at a restaurant. Then they saw a movie.

Brian had a busy day today. This morning he fixed his car. Then he cleaned his yard. This afternoon he planted flowers, and then he washed his windows. This evening he read the newspaper, and he wrote to his brother. Then he took a bath.

Chapter 17 – Page 163

Listen and choose the correct answer.

1. Before we bought Captain Crispy Cereal, we were always sick. Now we're always healthy.
2. We bought new chairs for our living room because our old chairs were very uncomfortable. We love our new chairs. They're VERY comfortable.
3. My daughter Lucy didn't finish her milk this morning. She wasn't very thirsty.
4. Fred was very upset this morning. He was late for the bus, and he didn't get to work on time.
5. Hmm. Where are Peter and Mary? They were at work yesterday, but they aren't here today.
6. Our kitchen floor was very dull. Our neighbors recommended Sparkle Floor Wax, and now our kitchen floor isn't dull any more. It's shiny!

Side by Side Gazette – Page 165

Listen and match the products.

ANNOUNCER: And now a word from our sponsors.

WOMAN: I had a problem with my teeth. They were very yellow, and I was upset. I went to my dentist, and she recommended Dazzle. So I went to the store and I bought some. Now I brush my teeth with Dazzle every day. My teeth aren't yellow any more. They're white. They're VERY white! Thank you, Dazzle!

ANNOUNCER: Are YOUR teeth yellow? Try Dazzle today!

TED: Bob! This kitchen floor is beautiful!
BOB: Thanks, Ted.
TED: Is it new?
BOB: Oh, no! This is my old kitchen floor.
TED: But it's so shiny!
BOB: That's right, Ted. It IS shiny, because I bought Shiny-Time!
TED: Shiny-Time?
BOB: Yes. Shiny-Time!
ANNOUNCER: That's right, Ted. YOU can have a shiny kitchen floor, too. Use Shiny-Time . . . every time!

WOMAN: Alan? What's the matter?
MAN: I don't know. I jog all the time, but today I'm really tired. Tell me, Julie, you're NEVER tired. You're always energetic. How do you do it?
WOMAN: Energy Plus!
MAN: Energy Plus?
WOMAN: Yes, Alan, Energy Plus! Before I bought Energy Plus, I was always tired like you. But now I'm energetic all the time!
ANNOUNCER: Tired? Try Energy Plus today! You can find it in supermarkets and drug stores everywhere.

PRESIDENT: Thank you. Thank you very much.
ASSISTANT: That was excellent, Mr. President.
PRESIDENT: Thank you, Ron. You know, I have a terrible sore throat.
ASSISTANT: I can hear that, Mr. President. Here. Try one of these.
PRESIDENT: What are they?
ASSISTANT: Lucky Lemon Drops.
PRESIDENT: Lucky Lemon Drops?
ASSISTANT: Yes, Mr. President. They're really good for a sore throat.
PRESIDENT: Thanks, Ron.
ANNOUNCER: Lucky Lemon Drops. They're good for the president! They're good for you!

WOMAN: My dog's fur was dull. It was VERY dull, and my dog was very sad. Then I bought K-9 Shine! Yes, K-9 Shine. I washed my dog with K-9 Shine, and now his fur is shiny! It's very shiny, and my dog is very happy!
ANNOUNCER: Try K-9 Shine today! YOUR dog's fur can be shiny, too!

Cardinal Numbers

1	one	20	twenty
2	two	21	twenty-one
3	three	22	twenty-two
4	four	.	.
5	five	.	.
6	six	29	twenty-nine
7	seven	30	thirty
8	eight	40	forty
9	nine	50	fifty
10	ten	60	sixty
11	eleven	70	seventy
12	twelve	80	eighty
13	thirteen	90	ninety
14	fourteen	100	one hundred
15	fifteen	200	two hundred
16	sixteen	.	.
17	seventeen	.	.
18	eighteen	900	nine hundred
19	nineteen	1,000	one thousand
		2,000	two thousand
		.	.
		10,000	ten thousand
		100,000	one hundred thousand
		1,000,000	one million

Irregular Verbs: Past Tense

be	was
begin	began
buy	bought
do	did
drink	drank
drive	drove
eat	ate
forget	forgot
get	got
go	went
grow	grew
have	had
make	made
meet	met
read	read
ride	rode
see	saw
sing	sang
sit	sat
steal	stole
take	took
write	wrote

Index